# SALVAGE YOUR SUPER

## Money-making strategies for financing your future — at any age

Geoff Peck

First published 2009 by Wrightbooks
an imprint of John Wiley & Sons Australia, Ltd
42 McDougall Street, Milton Qld 4064

Office also in Melbourne

Typeset in Berkeley LT 11/14pt



National Library of Australia Cataloguing-in-Publication entry:

| | |
|---|---|
| Author: | Peck, Geoff. |
| Title: | Salvage your super: Money-making strategies for financing your future — at any age / Geoff Peck. |
| ISBN: | 9781742169477 (pbk.) |
| Notes: | Includes index. |
| Subjects: | Finance, Personal — Australia.<br>Finance, Personal — Planning.<br>Saving and investment — Australia.<br>Stocks — Australia.<br>Investments — Australia. |
| Dewey Number: | 332.0240994 |



Cover design by Studio 131

Cover images © iStockphoto.com/hidesy and iStockphoto.com/LPETTET.

Printed in Australia by McPherson's Printing Group

10 9 8 7 6 5 4 3 2 1

**Disclaimer**

The material in this publication is of the nature of general comment only, and does not represent professional advice. It is not intended to provide specific guidance for particular circumstances and it should not be relied on as the basis for any decision to take action or not take action on any matter which it covers. Readers should obtain professional advice where appropriate, before making any such decision. To the maximum extent permitted by law, the author and publisher disclaim all responsibility and liability to any person, arising directly or indirectly from any person taking or not taking action based upon the information in this publication.

# Contents

# About the author

Geoff Peck has worked in the Australian superannuation industry since 1985. In that time he has held senior roles in product development, administration, distribution and general management, culminating in the role of Head of Superannuation Solutions for BT Financial Group, which manages superannuation and pension assets of more than $14 billion.

Geoff has extensive experience in all areas of superannuation, life insurance and investment and is committed to helping people to better understand their superannuation arrangements and thereby maximise its value.

Geoff retired from full-time work in 2006 to spend more time with his young children and be actively involved in the most 'fun' part of their upbringing. Recently relocated to a seaside town on the far north coast of New South Wales, Geoff now has a role as a non-executive director for a life insurance company and is an active campaigner for the Smith Family's financial literacy program.

# Acknowledgements

Throughout this book I have used data and charts that have been provided by some good friends within the superannuation industry: Warren Chant and Andrea West from Chant West Financial Services; Michael Rice from Rice Warner; Linda Elkins from Russell Investments; Nicolette Rubinsztein from Colonial First State; and Michaela McGlynn and Chris Caton from BT Financial Group. I would like to thank all of them for the help and support that they have provided.

Special thanks must also go to Melinda Howes for all of her great suggestions on the early drafts and to Mary Masters for helping me through the process of writing this book.

# Preface

This is a little book about super, but more importantly it is a book about super that has been written after one of the most disastrous periods for investment markets. The Global Financial Crisis will have after-effects that take years to work through our investments and this event has had an important impact on our superannuation balances.

This book should be able to help make some sense of those impacts, and also help with some strategies to get your super working again. If you were lucky enough not to have been affected by the Global Financial Crisis, there are some great ideas on how to capitalise on opportunities that have been created as a result of investment markets being revalued.

While 2008 was important in many ways, it is a year that should also be thought of as simply part of the investment cycle. There is good news here as well as some telling lessons.

My own situation and experience has some bearing on why this book was written. I have worked for over 20 years in the superannuation industry and I retired from full-time work in 2006. Prior to retiring I was the Head of Superannuation for BT Financial Group — one of the largest providers of superannuation and investment products in the country. I now work part time as a non-executive director of a life insurance company while bringing up my two young children.

As an expert in superannuation, my challenge will be to keep the simple core messages in plain sight. As a warning for any superannuation experts reading this book, there are areas of complexity that I have purposely avoided or ignored because they simply add no value to the non-experts' ability to manage their super better. My goal is to help non-experts take an interest and manage their super in a fundamentally better way.

Like many Australians, I felt very comfortable about my financial situation in the lead up to the events of 2008. My superannuation and other investments had done incredibly well over the previous years, to the point where I could retire early. Being a fundamental believer in long-term investment strategies, I didn't change my investments as 2008 unfolded. I stayed fully committed to shares — and rode the train down into the valley of doom.

I see myself in that group of Australians in the middle of their working lives. My wife and I are still at least 15 to 20 years away from full retirement. We had children late in our lives and they will be dependent on us for the same period — maybe even longer.

My parents are in their mid 70s. While they receive a part Age Pension they are heavily reliant on their self funded superannuation pension. As a result of 2008 they have recently experienced real stress over their financial security. My wife's parents are in their mid 60s and were thinking about how to retire. Their decisions were also affected by the events of 2008. In both cases they found ways to deal with these events.

I also look at people starting out in their careers. There are good reasons why people in their 20s and 30s shouldn't be worried about what happened in 2008, and in fact this has created some fantastic opportunities for them.

The concerns and issues of all of these groups will be addressed within the strategies described in this book. The case studies are realistic because they deal with the real life issues that I know are affecting people in different age groups.

## Introduction to the wonderful world of superannuation

As this is a book about how to save your superannuation, it is worth spending a little bit of time on why your superannuation is worth saving.

Superannuation is one of the most broadly used ways of investing money in Australia and yet remains one of the most misunderstood. Almost every working Australian has at least one superannuation account. Unfortunately many Australians have far more than one superannuation account, and this is a clear indicator of how poorly managed our superannuation assets are.

Superannuation is an incredibly complicated animal if you want to become an expert, but at its core is something that is really quite simple: superannuation is a low-taxed investment.

As a user of superannuation you don't need to know the fine details of the tax complexities generated by decades of government tinkering. You don't need to know the intricacies of how the preservation system works and the interaction of a host of related pieces of legislation. Just think of it as a low-taxed investment with one major trade-off compared to other investments: *you can't use the money until you retire.*

## Superannuation is necessary

In the early 1980s the Australian Government responded to the warnings of economic and social catastrophe that awaited our country once the baby boomers started to retire. At the time, most Australians had to rely on the Age Pension once they retired, as superannuation was only offered to a small part of the population — primarily those who worked in larger companies.

The warnings concerned what would happen when a bunch of related factors started to gang up and mug an entire generation. The Age Pension is essentially funded by taxes — primarily income tax. In the 1980s there were six working Australians paying tax for every pensioner on the Age Pension. It was estimated that this ratio would drop to three working Australians for every pensioner by the year 2030. The combination of massive extra need for pension dollars with massive reduction in income tax funding as a proportion of that need meant that the government had to find an alternative to the Age Pension.

Superannuation was chosen as the saviour. The superannuation system was extensively revised and massively broadened in terms of access. In 1992, the Superannuation Guarantee legislation came into effect, such that pretty much every employed Australian was receiving superannuation contributions.

Given that superannuation was compulsory and that it was the chosen vehicle to help Australians fund their own retirement, the government wanted to ensure that it was effective. They made sure that the tax that applies to superannuation was lower than for most other forms of investment. The primary reason for this was to ensure that people's superannuation balances would grow faster.

With these tax concessions came a trade-off. If superannuation was the chosen investment for retirement purposes and we receive tax concessions to make it work better, the government wanted to ensure that it wasn't used for anything other than retirement. Fair enough.

Now there are a couple of ways superannuation can be accessed prior to retirement, but as a general rule they aren't particularly attractive circumstances: death, permanent disability or severe financial hardship. This book is not designed to address these events and if you need advice on these situations then you should contact your superannuation fund for specific help.

We now enjoy one of the most modern and well-funded retirement systems in the world—to the point where other countries are modelling their retirement systems on ours.

While superannuation is concessionally taxed it is sometimes hard to work out why. As a result, many of us don't appreciate our superannuation as an investment opportunity. By better understanding the tax breaks, we will use it more and get more out of our investment dollars. It is therefore worth spending a bit of time on a couple of important tax elements of our superannuation system. We get tax breaks on the contributions we make to superannuation, the investment earnings that accrue before we reach retirement age are also given a tax break, and once we retire both the investment earnings of the super account and the income we receive out of our super are tax free.

The various components of superannuation—contributions and earnings—are taxed at a maximum rate of 15 per cent. This means that if you have a marginal tax rate of more than 15 per cent then superannuation represents a low-tax investment for you.

Another thing to remember about tax is that the superannuation fund is the thing that is taxed, not the person. This makes superannuation very simple to use. We don't have to declare superannuation investment earnings as part of our annual tax return. In fact, the only complication to our personal tax situation as a result of having superannuation can occur when we make extra contributions that qualify for a government-funded matching contribution. Yes, in some circumstances the government will also contribute to your superannuation account as well!

## Superannuation versus all other investments

It is worth having a quick think about the obvious investments that most of us use. For many Australians, the top of mind investments start with residential investment properties and then move to specific company shares. Superannuation generally comes up only after they think about it for a little while.

Superannuation is actually a difficult investment to compare to other more traditional investments. This is not because we don't have enough information on the superannuation fund but rather because we don't get sufficient information on all other investments to make a valid comparison.

If you ask someone how their specific company share investment has gone, you generally get told the purchase price of the shares and the current share price. While this gives you some idea of performance, it ignores the length of time the shares have been held and the dividend returns that have been received. It also ignores the trading costs of buying and selling the shares, and any additional accounting costs for holding the shares and properly recording all of this in the individual's income tax return.

The superannuation investment performance numbers that you see quoted on your superannuation statements or in the financial papers are on an *after-tax and after-fee* basis. Performance for almost every other investment is quoted on a *pre-tax and pre-fee* basis. So in order to make a proper performance comparison between superannuation investments and non-superannuation investments, you need to make an allowance for the tax and fees that you would pay by investing in the non-superannuation investments.

*Warning: rant about investment property to follow . . .*

For decades, Australians have loved to invest in residential property—a tradition that has seemingly been passed down through the generations. However, despite its very extensive use, disclosure of the fees and costs associated with investing in property is virtually non-existent in comparison to superannuation. The result is that very few owners of residential investment properties have an accurate understanding of the after-tax and after-costs investment performance of their property.

How many times have you been at a dinner party or barbecue and been confronted by that friend who happily announces that her investment property has doubled in value since she bought it? She doesn't seem to mention how long that doubling took, the high fees and duties with getting in to and out of the investment, the renovations and maintenance that she had to lavish on the property during her ownership or the tax that is yet to be paid when she does sell it.

*End of rant.*

## Types of superannuation funds

It is also worth considering what type of superannuation fund you have. Superannuation does come in different flavours. The reasons are partly historical and partly needs driven, but the end result is that we all have a choice of superannuation funds in terms of cost, service, advice and investment flexibility. If you want something that has high levels of investment flexibility and built-in financial advice then you may want to look at some retail fund arrangements. If you want something that is simpler, cheaper and more personally manageable then a large industry fund may be more appropriate. If you are part of a large employer group you may have access to all of these things at a low cost.

Industry funds currently do a lot of promotion around the concept that they are cheaper and don't pay commissions. This is generally true when comparing industry funds to retail funds, but if you are in a large corporate fund, public sector fund or part of a large employer group in an employer master trust you are almost certainly in a fund that offers similar benefits in terms of low fees and no commissions.

One of the strategies that we look at in later sections of the book is consolidation of your superannuation accounts. The objective of this strategy is to move all of your various superannuation accounts into one main superannuation account—and to do that you need to start by understanding what type of superannuation accounts you currently use.

The main types of superannuation in Australia are:

- *corporate and government funds.* Large employers in both the private and public sectors may have a superannuation fund just for their employees. These are generally quite large funds and often provide their members with low-cost and generous benefits.
- *industry funds.* Different industry groups established these funds in the 1980s and 1990s to offer employees in their particular industry a low-cost superannuation account. These funds are now often open to people from any industry.
- *retail superannuation funds.* These are primarily offered by superannuation providers such as large insurance and wealth management companies. These accounts generally have higher fees than corporate and industry funds, but the fees often include the cost of financial advice—even if you don't use it.
- *employer superannuation master trust.* These funds are a crossover between corporate and retail funds. Many of the same companies that provide retail superannuation funds also offer a group arrangement for the employees of specific companies. The costs can vary, generally depending upon the size of the group. Employees of larger companies using a master trust can enjoy fees that are similar to industry and corporate super funds (especially once life insurance costs are taken into account) whereas employees of

smaller companies will have fees that are similar to retail arrangements.

⇨ *self managed superannuation funds (SMSFs)*. These funds are set up for individual family groups and the members are also the trustees of the fund. As a general rule you need three things to make these funds viable:

- assets of at least $250 000—otherwise the fund can be very expensive compared to alternatives
- specific and sophisticated investment strategies and needs
- a thorough understanding of the superannuation environment and obligations, as members are also trustees and are responsible for the fund meeting all of its regulatory requirements.

## Predicting future returns and outcomes

At various stages of this book, there will be comments about expected investment returns and outcomes. When you develop strategies for the future you must make assumptions about how those strategies will play out—what sort of outcomes can you expect if you use one strategy versus another? Wherever possible the assumed rates of returns used are consistent with the assumptions used by the Australian Securities & Investments Commission (ASIC) in their superannuation and pension calculators that are on ASIC's FIDO website.

The investment performance assumptions used in those projections are based on the historical performance of all of the major investment asset classes: cash, fixed interest, property and shares. The long-term investment performance for each of these asset classes is then used to calculate a projected superannuation balance, taking into account the ratio of these different asset classes.

As cash has the lowest long-term investment performance, the more cash you have in your superannuation investments the lower the projected superannuation balance will be. In our projections we assume that cash will produce 5.5 per cent per annum before fees and tax. Conversely, as shares have the highest long-term performance, the more of this asset class you have the higher the end balance will be. We assume that shares will produce 9 per cent per annum before fees and tax over the long term.

While this sounds reasonably straightforward, we also know that investing in shares does not produce a constant flow of 9 per cent annual returns. In some years it will be very high and in other years it will be low, and in a very small number of years we will get a horror result like 2008. The key to this is to think about the returns as an average. In order to do this, you must have a time frame that is consistent with that average.

We know 2008 was a horror year, but the preceding five years were fantastic. Part of the reason that we lost so much out of our superannuation accounts in 2008 was that we had more to lose due to the stellar performance of the previous years. Given the long time frame of your superannuation, you shouldn't look at the bad years or the stellar years in isolation, rather you have to look at the performance in terms of decades. Figure 0.1 (overleaf) shows how shares can perform over the long term.

We need to acknowledge that bad years happen, but equally that they are part of the reason we have stellar years as well.

**Figure 0.1: All Ordinaries Accumulation Index, 1979 to 2008**

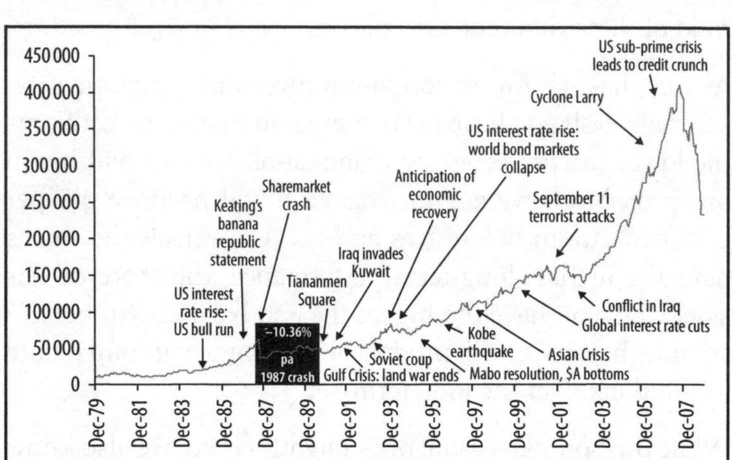


*Source:* Data to 31 December 2008. IRESS chart shows the value of $10 000 invested on 31/12/79, S&P/ASX All Ordinaries Accumulation Index/Colonial First State.

The collapse of 2008 has provided another lesson about value. In a normal investment environment, the price of a share in a company is largely about an educated guess as to the future prospects of that company. It is effectively the price that someone is prepared to pay to own a piece of that company's future income and growth prospects.

The most important part of that last paragraph are the words 'in a normal investment environment'. What makes predicting short-term sharemarket performance hard is the fact that these markets experience substantial periods where the environment is anything but 'normal'. Sharemarkets operate in cycles, and one of the most powerful cycles is the human-driven one of fear and greed. The cycle is shown in figure 0.2.

The best way to deal with this type of occurrence is to acknowledge it, know that you can't predict it, and to develop and stick to a strategy that takes this into account.

**Figure 0.2: sharemarket cycle**

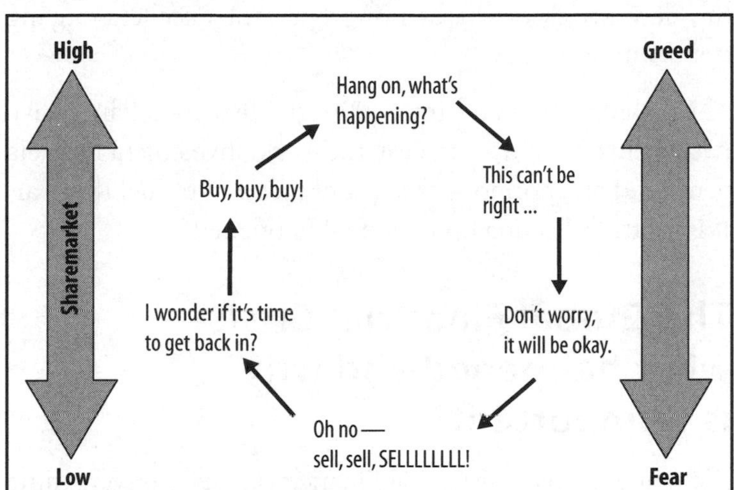


One of the other components of this human cycle is the way the fear is spread. For most of us, our main source of information on what the investment markets are doing is the nightly TV news. We might also see something about it in the morning papers. There are two important aspects of this media.

The first is to acknowledge that there are different levels of quality of the information and analysis that we see. A good guide to this quality is to see where and how much of the news bulletin is regularly devoted to financial matters. If the news program that you watch normally puts the finance report after the sport and just before the weather, then you have a sense of how important finance is perceived to be.

The second point is that, ultimately, bad news is more newsworthy than good news. Dramatic falls in world sharemarkets make for a better news story if they are coupled with analysis of how many billions of dollars have been wiped off the balances of pensioners, rather than whether the new prices of shares now represent excellent buying opportunities.

Throughout 2008 and into 2009, the fear merchants have had a field day, and let's face it, the world investment markets generated an enormous amount of material to fuel this fear. It is worth reflecting on how it all happened.

## The Global Financial Crisis—what happened and why is it important?

For many people, the Global Financial Crisis was something that was affecting world sharemarkets but didn't really affect them. It really hit home though when they received their annual statement from their superannuation fund in the second half of 2008. For the first time in years, people saw their superannuation go backwards—a lot.

Even though many of us don't take an active interest in our superannuation, through it we are investors in the world's sharemarkets. Through our superannuation we own companies not just in Australia, but around the world. When a big, ugly sharemarket event occurs, our superannuation is one of the things that is impacted.

A year like 2008 will generate enormous amounts of analysis as to the root causes. Political aspirants use events like this to push their own agenda, further muddying the waters of why it happened. The reasons are many, and just as importantly the interaction of many elements also had a role to play.

While the roots of the Global Financial Crisis can be argued, the first concrete problems started to emerge in the middle of 2007 when the sub-prime mortgage problems in the US became apparent. Sub-prime mortgages are in effect home mortgages that were provided to people who had a higher risk of not being able to pay back their home loans—hence the term 'sub-prime'. The ultimate examples of these were termed 'NINJA' loans—no income, no job or assets. Even without the benefit of hindsight, loans of this type clearly have potential problems for both borrower and lender.

Adding to the mix of problems was the rise of collateralised debt obligations, or CDOs. A CDO, put simply, is an investment vehicle that packages up a lot of loans. The loans in question can be pretty much any form of debt security—credit card debt, personal finance debt, or in this case sub-prime home mortgages.

The CDO manager creates the investment vehicle and promotes the investment by claiming that it will provide a high investment return. Investors who are looking for a higher return than cash can provide may look at this type of investment with interest. They buy units in the CDO. The borrowers pay their interest each month, and these interest payments (after fees and profits taken by the CDO manager) are the income return of the CDO investors. While the borrowers are all paying their interest payments, there is no problem.

Complicating this is something called a secondary CDO. This is another investment vehicle, but unlike the CDO that invests in the book of loans, these secondary CDOs invest in *other* CDOs. In effect this can massively dilute the value of the underlying assets of the secondary CDO.

When the US housing market started to collapse in early 2007, mortgage owners started to default on their payments. This caused a spiralling effect that created situations where many home owners found that they owned homes where the mortgage was actually bigger than the value of the house, thus generating even more mortgage defaults. This gave rise to another great new term associated with the sub-prime mess: 'jingle mail'. In some cases, banks started to report situations where home owners would pack up all of their belongings, move out, and simply send the house keys to the bank.

As the defaults flowed through into the CDOs the CDO managers had to reduce what they paid out in terms of income. The secondary CDOs started to receive no income at all and the whole system started to collapse.

Certain investment banks that had developed and promoted these products started to realise the problems that they had with these products. They in turn started to declare significantly increasing exposure to these sub-prime mortgage products and CDOs. As a result, they had to start revaluing these assets downwards as they realised that the income streams were reducing or disappearing. Some of the asset revaluations were dramatic and caused massive writedowns in company balance sheets, and therefore huge losses were being declared.

Other banks in turn started to worry about lending further money to these investment banks. Credit within and between the financial services companies started to dry up and that in turn flowed through to lending to other businesses. Added to all of this was some very high profile company collapses in the US, and then massive government-funded bailouts of major financial institutions in the US, UK and Europe.

The world sharemarkets were going south in a big way as each month of 2008 brought more bad news of downgraded profit estimates or company collapses. Economists massively reduced their estimates of world growth, to a point where the general consensus was that a worldwide recession was virtually unavoidable. Consumer and business confidence went through the floor, further adding to the sense of panic.

The Australian Government and Reserve Bank — along with other governments around the world — went to great lengths to try to cushion the blow with bank deposit guarantees, massive public spending initiatives and interest rate cuts, all designed to stimulate the economy. Despite this effort, the sharemarkets in 2008 experienced one of the worst performance years on record.

At the time that the writing of this book finished in early March 2009, sharemarkets around the world are still falling. While the Australian sharemarket index — the S&P/ASX 200 — fell 38 per cent during 2008, the bigger story is the scope of the fall from its high in November 2007. By March 2009 that fall was nearly 54 per cent.

In the US, the story was even worse. The Dow Jones Index had fallen nearly 60 per cent and most experts expected it to go lower. Interest rates in the US were at 0.5 per cent per annum — record lows. The government was starting to run out of ways to support the economy, with no room to lower interest rates and record budget deficits.

By early March 2009 it was not apparent that the sharemarket bottom had been reached. The general consensus from Australian economists and fund managers at the time is that a recovery — at least in Australia — has a 50/50 chance of happening before the end of 2009; however, the US could take much longer and that may delay market recoveries elsewhere around the world. Time will tell.

Sharemarkets do tend to look ahead of economic conditions—usually by around six months. Sharemarkets therefore have an enormous amount of bad news factored into the company valuations. The sharemarkets in early 2009 reflected and expected the world economy to get worse before it got better. That said, further major sharemarket shocks, such as a major car company going broke, could inject further panic into sharemarkets around the world.

In times like this we often look to the past to give us some guidance on how the future may unfold. But the past is never an accurate predictor of the future, and this particular situation is different both subtly and profoundly in certain ways. But some of the lessons from the past that you may be able to apply to this situation are:

- Every recession ends.
- You won't know when until after it has happened.

The strategies outlined in this book do assume that the above two points will hold true.

Any book about superannuation must also be a book about investment. Having an understanding and regard to investment markets will help with the development of strategies that will help you get your superannuation back on track.

During times of such turmoil and uncertainty, surviving companies can be found to have significant potential value within their share prices. How we capitalise on this opportunity, or not, could make a big difference to the success of our future superannuation benefits.

## The 2009 Federal Budget

This book was written before the 2009 Federal Budget was read in the lower house of parliament on 12 May 2009.

However, due to the expectation that this Budget could contain potentially significant changes to superannuation and Age Pension benefits, we delayed finalising the book just in case some major spanners came out. Fortunately, while changes did occur, they were not as deep or broad as expected.

It may take some time for the Budget announcements to be debated in both houses of parliament before eventual passing into law, therefore we cannot know for certain that all of the announcements will become reality. However, once law reforms are passed the changes will be reflected in the online resources referenced in this book, therefore your personal calculations will always be up-to-date.

The main changes that will affect your superannuation and retirement income are:

- ⇨ The maximum Age Pension will be increased for both single and couple pensioners with the maximum single Age Pension going up to $16 504 per annum and the couple Age Pension to $25 274 per annum combined. These amounts will be indexed from 20 September 2009.
- ⇨ The Age Pension eligibility income test will be changed to reduce Age Pension entitlements if you are earning some income from other sources. The asset test will not be changed. For people that are already receiving part Age Pensions there will be transitional arrangements put in place to ease the impact of these changes.
- ⇨ The federal government plans to increase the Age Pension commencement age to 67. This change will be phased in between 2017 and 2023 and so will affect anyone born after 1952. Many of the

calculations in this book have been based on a 'notional' retirement age of 65, but you can check your Age Pension commencement date online at the Centrelink website <www.centrelink.com.au>.

- The maximum amount of concessionally taxed superannuation contributions—including both your superannuation guarantee contributions and any pre-tax or salary sacrifice contributions—will be lowered to a $25 000 annual limit from 1 July 2009. The contribution limit for after-tax contributions of $150 000 a year has not been changed. The reduced contribution limit does not affect any of the case studies used in this book.
- There will be a temporary reduction in the government co-contribution benefit for five years from 1 July 2009. The government co-contribution will drop from $1.50 for every dollar that you put in (with a maximum co-contribution of $1500) to $1.00 (with a maximum co-contribution of $1000) from 1 July 2009 until 30 June 2012. It will be increased to $1.25 (with a maximum co-contribution of $1250) from 1 July 2012 until 30 June 2014, and will return back up to the current rate after 1 July 2014.

While the changes to the Age Pension and temporary reduction in the government co-contribution scheme will slightly change some of the numbers coming out of some of the case studies, it will only cause a small change to your total retirement income. The most important thing to note is that the changes that have been announced do not change any of the principles or strategies outlined in this book.

# Chapter 1

## The four things that really make super work

One of the great things about superannuation is that there are some really simple and very powerful attributes to making it work really well as an investment. Unfortunately, there are also a few things that we can do that can get in the way.

There are four really important drivers that make a serious difference as to how well your superannuation will serve you in retirement:

- time
- type of investment
- tactics
- tariffs.

The first three are powers of good, and the last one can be a power of evil.

You may be surprised that there isn't a 'how much you contribute' component. Clearly, you will have a higher superannuation account balance if you put more in, but if you get control over the above four real powers then you will have to put much less in. The amount you need to contribute is actually a consequence of how well you manage your superannuation—not the other way around.

Equally, there are many of us that will need to top up our superannuation. If we have had broken work patterns due to raising children for example, or if we didn't have access to superannuation for our entire working life, extra contributions may well be the only way that we can build our superannuation to a level that will support us in retirement. We cover this in more detail in chapters 4 and 5.

## Time

Time is the most important factor in the accumulation of wealth—used wisely, time will reduce how much you have to contribute to superannuation and it will help you manage risk. Due to this, the structure of this book has been divided into different strategies for investing in different stages of life. These stages are framed around how far away you are from retirement. The strategies for each stage vary because of the power of time.

As an example of how powerful time can be, let's consider people born after 1970. The superannuation guarantee system was introduced in 1992, meaning that these people have most of their working life with at least 9 per cent of their annual salary going into a superannuation fund. Despite this, if they ignore their superannuation completely, make no additional contributions and leave the money invested in their default investment option (usually a balanced investment) they will more than likely have sufficient superannuation to maintain an income in retirement of only around 50 per cent of their pre-retirement income.

If these people invested in a high-growth investment option rather than the default balanced option over the full 40 years of their working life, then their superannuation benefit would most likely be 25 per cent more than if they had left the money in the default option.

You might be concerned that there is higher risk with this approach, especially in light of the Global Financial Crisis, but having time up your sleeve changes the way we look at risk. If you are now 40 or older you may be gnashing your teeth in frustration, because you didn't use compound interest in this way when you were younger, but don't worry, there are ways that you can still use it to your advantage.

The first way that you can benefit from compound interest is to buy another copy of this book for each of your adult children, highlight or dog ear this page and give it to your child and say, 'Read this'. If your mum or dad has given you this book and you have now read this page — don't just stop here, go to chapter 3 and read more about what you can do to plan for your retirement!

The second way you can benefit from compound interest is to remember that superannuation doesn't retire when you do! It has two stages of investment — the first is the contribution stage which runs up to your retirement, and the second is the draw down stage where you take out some of your superannuation each year to pay for your living costs in retirement.

Financial planners tend to think of short-term investments as those where you plan to use the money in less than two years. Medium-term investments are those that will get used in two to seven years, and long-term investments are basically everything else: longer than seven years.

Even if you are retired, you probably have more than 10 years left of active investing, and compound interest still has time to work for you. You will effectively need to think about your pension assets as having short-, medium- and long-term components. The next couple of years of pension payments need to be held in short-term investments, the following five or so in medium-term, and the remainder can be thought of as long-term investments.

*Nerd moment:* Albert Einstein spent a lot of his life working on the interaction of time with other aspects of the universe. It is claimed that while he was having a rest from working up the theory of relativity he had a look at how time and investments might interact. Compound interest was the answer, and Einstein ranked this as the most powerful force in the universe. The story may be apocryphal, but the fact is that compound interest over a long time frame can have a very significant effect on investment outcomes.

## Type of investment

The next power for good is the type of investment you use. Most superannuation funds will segment their investment options into one of six or so categories based on a risk versus return profile:

- *Cash:* 100 per cent invested in cash or similar securities.
- *Conservative:* Approximately 30 per cent invested in growth-style investments (Australian shares, international shares and property) and 70 per cent

invested in income-style investments (cash, Australian fixed interest or bonds and international fixed interest).

- *Moderately conservative:* Approximately 50 per cent invested in growth-style investments and 50 per cent invested in income-style investments.
- *Balanced:* Approximately 70 per cent invested in growth-style investments and 30 per cent invested in income-style investments.
- *Growth:* Approximately 85 per cent invested in growth-style investments and 15 per cent invested in income-style investments.
- *High growth:* Approximately 95 per cent invested in growth-style investments. Some small amounts of cash may exist as a result of cash flow requirements.

Funds differ in how they describe their options. Some funds will call 50 per cent growth/50 per cent income a balanced option, while other funds will call 70 per cent growth/ 30 per cent income a balanced option. The important thing is the amount of growth assets (shares or property) versus the amount of income or defensive assets (fixed interest and cash), rather than the name of the investment option. I have used the asset allocations shown above for all projections in this book.

Even if your superannuation fund offers you 100 or more investment options the fund disclosure material will generally relate many of those options back to one of these six categories. The basic rule of thumb here is that the more you move towards the high-growth end of this spectrum, the higher your superannuation balance will be *if you are investing over a time frame of at least 10 years.*

The trade-off for this higher performance is higher risk.

'Risk' in superannuation funds is managed through diversification. If we go back to looking at our six main categories, the high-growth option will generally be considered the 'riskiest'. A high-growth option will be invested almost exclusively in the shares of a combination of Australian and international companies. But there is still diversification here due to the high number of individual companies that make up all of the companies within this investment option. Its volatility will be higher than the other options. It will have the ability to produce higher returns in good years and negative returns in bad years.

At the other end of the scale, the cash option will almost never post a negative return, but it has very limited ability to deliver after-tax returns much above inflation over the long term.

If you look at the historical returns of the six types of investments over different periods (shown in table 1.1) you start to get a sense of these differences.

You can see the impact of the Global Financial Crisis in table 1.1. These performance results are measured at the end of 2008 so they include most of the investment damage that this crisis caused. The 10-year numbers show that more conservative options outperformed the higher growth options, but once you move out to 15-year numbers that starts to change.

*Generally* the more growth assets your investments contain, the higher return you will receive over the long term. Table 1.1 is historical — backward looking. For projections we need to use an estimate of investment performance in the future. The projections used in our case studies (shown in table 1.2) use estimated future investment performance supplied by ASIC.

### Table 1.1: historical returns

| | Aust. shares | Int. shares | 90% growth | 70% growth | 30% growth | Cash |
|---|---|---|---|---|---|---|
| 29-year pa compound | 11.7% | 10.8% | 11.6% | 11.6% | 10.9% | 9.0% |
| 20-year pa compound | 9.1% | 6.0% | 8.3% | 8.7% | 8.8% | 7.3% |
| 15-year pa compound | 7.8% | 4.4% | 6.8% | 7.2% | 7.1% | 6.0% |
| 10-year pa compound | 7.0% | −1.9% | 4.0% | 4.8% | 5.9% | 5.8% |

Returns are gross (before tax and fees) for period to 31 December 2008.
*Source:* Russell Investments — *Risk vs Return* 2009 edition.

### Table 1.2: return projections

| Investment option | Estimate of future long-term (10+ years) investment performance before tax and fees |
|---|---|
| High-growth option (95% growth assets) | 9.0% pa |
| Growth option (85% growth assets) | 8.5% pa |
| Balanced option (70% growth assets) | 8.0% pa |
| Conservative option (35% growth assets) | 6.0% pa |
| Capital stable or cash (0% growth assets) | 5.5% pa |

*Source:* FIDO and Chant West.

Most funds offer you not only a choice of investments around a risk and return profile, but also a choice of different fund managers and even individual company securities.

The important part of this is to realise that the choice you make here can make a very substantial difference to the end result you generate.

## Tactics

Okay, let's get this out of the way: sharemarket crashes happen. The effects of market corrections and crashes on our superannuation are manageable though, even if you are already retired or in the final years of your working life. The secret is knowing with absolute certainty that crashes will happen from time to time and also knowing that you don't know when. The only way to deal with this type of occurrence is to develop, and stick to, a strategy that takes this into account—you must have a tactic.

One of the worst things that you can do to eat away at superannuation funds is tinkering. Yes, that means *your* tinkering. As we will see in later chapters, there are some good strategies to help you get the most out of your super and it is important to review your strategies occasionally. However, the common theme of all investment strategies is to develop sound reasons for the strategy and then *stick with it.*

My father retired in 1986, and for many years his superannuation has been his only source of income. He received advice at the time he retired and has maintained an adviser ever since. The basic strategy was to keep the next two years of pension payments in cash and the remainder to be invested in a balanced fund. This has all worked very well for him over the years, but there have been times when he really struggled to stick with the strategy: 1987, 1994, 2001/02 and 2008 were all terrible years for sharemarket returns. During each of these years, he saw his superannuation balance go backwards, and the temptation to act on the media hype or 'advice' from friends and family is hard to ignore. Of course, this hype and 'advice' is almost always being delivered after the event. So the pressure to act, to switch out of sharemarket-linked investments, is usually happening after the damage has been done and usually just as the markets are starting to turn for the better.

Dad stuck with his strategy though, and as a result his superannuation has lasted much longer than he initially anticipated. Even after you take into account the sharemarket falls of 2008 and the corresponding negative return to his balanced investment option, he is ahead of where he thought he would be based on projections he did when he retired in 1986.

While it is fantastic that Australians are now paying more attention to their superannuation, this can sometimes lead to them doing more harm than good if they start to make changes that are not consistent with their well-thought-out strategies. Clearly, changes to the strategy will be appropriate from time to time, but generally not because of a neighbour's advice or a downturn in the investment markets.

As addressed in the section on time, superannuation is long term, so as an investor you can look through the fear and greed aspects of sharemarket cycles and invest in accordance with long-term performance principles.

The regular contributions of superannuation also allow you to use a concept called 'dollar cost averaging'. Dollar cost averaging comes out of regular investment. Let's say that your monthly superannuation contribution is $500. Every month, that money could be used to invest in a variety of investments, but let's say it is shares for demonstration purposes. As the money you invest each month remains the same, the amount of shares you buy will depend on the price of those shares. If the sharemarket is in an expensive stage of the cycle, then you will buy fewer shares, but when the market is in a cheap stage of the cycle, you actually buy more shares.

The hardest thing about using this simple approach is to ignore the doom and gloom that happens during the cheap stages of the cycle.

One of the world's most successful investors, Warren Buffett, once wrote: 'Be fearful when others are greedy and greedy when others are fearful'. Nathaniel Rothschild (third Baron of Rothschild) in a similar vein has been reported as saying: 'Buy when there is blood on the street—even if the blood is your own'.

The problem of course with both of these sentiments is that it is just as hard to pick the bottom of the sharemarket cycle as it is to pick the top. In effect, every investor is trying to buy low and sell high, and the vast bulk of evidence would suggest that very few people can do this consistently over the long term. Dollar cost averaging doesn't attempt to help you pick highs and lows. What it does is remove the wasted effort around trying to pick them and instead smoothes the investing process.

One thing we do know is that sharemarket corrections or crashes will happen from time to time. We also know that we can't predict when they will occur. We simply need to develop strategies that take these two facts into account and then stick to them.

## Tariffs

Tariffs such as taxes and fees act as a drag on investment performance. Despite this, we have to accept that these tariffs exist and will continue to do so.

Most people don't like to pay taxes, but equally most people accept they will have to and that it is appropriate for the maintenance of their society. There is also a clear desire to not pay more tax than they should. Importantly, you as a superannuation investor don't have to worry about this in respect of your superannuation investments, as it is the superannuation fund that is taxed and you can rest assured that the superannuation fund trustee is doing what it needs to do about minimising the tax the fund pays.

So while we need to recognise that tax is a drag on investment performance of superannuation funds, we should also recognise that because of the low-taxed environment superannuation funds enjoy, tax drag is less than what would apply to our investments if they were outside of superannuation.

Fees on the other hand are something that you can have some influence over. The easiest way to reduce fees is to have only one superannuation fund. Many Australians have more than one fund, usually as a result of changing jobs prior to the allowance of employee-nominated fund contributions, and each fund you collect will charge its own set of administration fees. Consolidating all of your superannuation funds into one and then requesting your employer to pay the ongoing contributions to that fund will almost certainly save you money. In addition, it will be much easier for you to then implement your superannuation strategies as you will only have to do it with one fund.

Further to this, there are now a couple of really good websites available that can help you compare your fund with other funds in terms of the fees and services offered. One of the best superannuation comparison tools is called Applecheck by Chant West. You can access this directly at <www.chantwest.com.au> or you may also be able to access it through your existing superannuation fund's website.

Importantly, when looking at fee comparisons you also need to look at the service and feature differences available. Some funds pride themselves on low cost, but that may mean that they offer a low service model as well. The other thing to keep in mind when comparing funds is that if you find out that your fund is expensive then that may be a result of additional services included in the cost.

Many retail superannuation funds are more expensive than industry superannuation funds or large corporate superannuation funds, however part of that additional expense may be that the retail fund fee will include the cost of some limited financial advice — it is up to you to make sure that you know about these fees and are using the services for which you are paying. While industry and corporate superannuation funds rarely include the cost of this service in their fees, they quite often can provide you with access to financial planners for an additional fee.

If you are reading this book then you must be interested in finding out more about your superannuation fund, and financial advice may very well be worthwhile. Financial advice can incorporate all of your wealth needs, or it can be limited to just your superannuation arrangements. In the latter case, the adviser would generally help you with your choice of superannuation fund, the investment options you should use and an appropriate level of life insurance cover. We look at some of the benefits of getting more detailed financial advice — and how to get it — in chapter 7.

# Chapter 2

## Your superannuation investment profile

One of the most important parts of developing a strategy in any area of endeavour is to first get an understanding of some of the parameters or constraints within which the strategy needs to work.

Investment is now something that many of us talk about with our family and friends. It has become a common dinner party or barbecue topic. It is only natural on hearing of a new investment strategy that we ask ourselves: I wonder if I should do that? The problem with a strategy that we hear about is that the strategy by itself may not take into account many of your individual circumstances and goals. In addition, while superannuation is an investment, it is an investment with very particular goals and time frames — both of which are often very different from the goals and time frames that your average dinner table investment strategy may have.

Using an investment strategy without first establishing clear investment goals is a bit like going on holiday without first working out where you want to go or what sort of holiday you want to have. Similarly, investing without a clear time frame would be like saying I want to go to the other side of the country for my holiday but I am not sure how long I have to get there. If you only have a week then you better not go on foot.

Within a book or any other form of general advice, it is virtually impossible to set out an investment strategy that completely and thoroughly takes into account all of your particular circumstances. Sitting down with a qualified financial planner may therefore be a very valuable and worthwhile exercise.

What we can do here though is go through some of the basics on how to understand your investment profile. This should help you understand the constraints that you may have in working out how to get to your retirement goals.

Superannuation will be a very important piece of your retirement strategy, but it won't be the only piece. Other resources that you may have will also need to be taken into account. These may include other investments, income from part-time work, social security entitlements and even your own house.

The easiest approach is to split the various strategies into time frames based on your current age. Time creates the biggest differences in terms of the strategies. In essence, you are looking at how long you have to go before you retire.

## How much will you need?

Before you launch into the strategies specific to your age group, you also need to think through what your retirement goals are. This is actually more involved than you may think. For some people retirement is simply not working any more, but the real question here is what sort of lifestyle do you want to have in retirement? Once you have a sense of this, you can then work out roughly what sort of income you need to maintain that lifestyle.

For example, if your retirement lifestyle is simply the same lifestyle you currently enjoy with an assumption that you won't be supporting a house mortgage in retirement, you can quite easily work out what that lifestyle costs in today's dollars. Simply take your current after-tax income, subtract the mortgage repayments and any regular investments that you make, and the result will be the after-tax income you need to maintain your current lifestyle.

You would also need to add in a budget for things that you don't spend money on every year, such as replacing cars, appliances or furniture. If you want a higher cost lifestyle, such as allowing for more travel or hobbies, then you need to add in the costs of these extra elements.

As a guide, table 2.1 (overleaf) can be used to help you estimate the cost of your desired lifestyle. This table is an approximation of the budget required for a couple to live a basic but comfortable lifestyle. It does not include an allowance for in-home care or aged services, which may be appropriate for later stages of retirement.

**Table 2.1: approximate budget required for a couple in retirement**

| Item | Replacement schedule | Cost ($) | Annual cost allowance ($) |
|---|---|---|---|
| **Living costs** | | | |
| Food | Weekly | 80 | 4 160 |
| Going out (pub, restaurants and shows) | Weekly | 100 | 5 200 |
| Hair, clothing and shoes | Monthly | 100 | 1 200 |
| Electricity, water and gas | Monthly | 325 | 3 900 |
| Council rates/services | Quarterly | 500 | 2 000 |
| Phone and online services | Monthly | 150 | 1 800 |
| Car (fuel, servicing and registration) | Annual | 5 000 | 5 000 |
| Medical, pharmaceutical and dental | Annual | 2 000 | 2 000 |
| Gifts (birthdays and Christmas) | Annual | 500 | 500 |
| Pet costs (worming, vaccinations, tick and fleas, kennel boarding, insurance) | Annual | 500 | 500 |
| **Insurance** | | | |
| Health | Annual | 2 000 | 2 000 |
| Home building and contents | Annual | 1 000 | 1 000 |
| Car | Annual | 1 000 | 1 000 |
| **Major items** | | | |
| Car replacements | 5 years | 25 000 | 5 000 |
| Computers and phones | 5 years | 2 000 | 400 |
| Household maintenance | Annual | 500 | 500 |
| House upgrades/renovations | 10 years | 100 000 | 10 000 |
| **Holidays and travel** | | | |
| Visiting family and friends | 6 monthly | 1 000 | 2 000 |
| Overseas | 5 years | 10 000 | 2 000 |
| **Hobbies and pastimes** | | | |
| Boat and fishing trips | Annual | 1 000 | 1 000 |
| Golf and sports memberships | Annual | 5 000 | 5 000 |
| Equipment replacement | Annual | 500 | 500 |
| Other hobby costs | Annual | 500 | 500 |
| **TOTAL** | **Annual** | | **57 160** |

Given that you are looking at a post-retirement phase, you should not have to allow for the costs of child care or education. Nor should you need to worry about insurance cover for your life or income protection. Clearly, these types of cover are very important while you are still working, but they are generally not going to be appropriate once you retire.

Once you have done this you will have a basic lifestyle cost in mind. Here are some examples:

- ⇨ A very basic lifestyle cost would be $30 000 per annum after tax. This might involve a part Age Pension and offer very limited ability to enjoy even inexpensive pastimes or travel.
- ⇨ A medium cost lifestyle might be $50 000 per annum after tax; this should afford an average Australian a modest but comfortable lifestyle.
- ⇨ If your tastes run to regular overseas holidays, eating out often, entertaining friends and family and club memberships then you may need $80 000 per annum after tax . . . or much, much more.

Don't forget that the cost of this lifestyle will increase every year due to inflation. Long-term inflation in Australia is projected to be around 3 per cent per annum. This doesn't sound like much but it means that your cost of living *doubles* every 23 years. Within the space of an average retirement, your medium-cost lifestyle of $50 000 at age 65 will be costing you $100 000 a year by the time you are 88.

The other expense that generally goes up as you get older is your health-care costs. Ill health could mean that even a modest retirement lifestyle may require a very large amount of money to secure.

## How long does it have to last?

The equation for determining whether you have enough money in retirement is a function of your available assets, your lifestyle costs and how long you will live.

The Australian Bureau of Statistics and the Institute of Actuaries of Australia prepare life expectancy tables for use by the insurance and retirement industries. These tables are updated regularly and also take into account information gathered at each National Census. The table given here reflects the life expectancy of males and females of different ages generated from statistics taken during the years 2000 to 2002. A more up to date set of life expectancies is now available but at the time of writing is not yet used in the calculators referenced in later chapters. In order to maintain consistency with the projections produced by these calculators, I have shown the 2002 life expectancy table.

The firm trend of these updates is that more Australians are living longer. The table here shows a male who is now 65 has a life expectancy of 17.7 years, a female currently aged 65 can expect to live for 21.2 years or through to age 86. Every time these tables have been updated over the last century, these numbers go up. The 2005 tables show these numbers as 18.5 years for males and 21.6 years for females. So if you are currently 40 years old, you may find that your life expectancy once you reach retirement is three to five years longer than the numbers shown here for people that are currently 65.

Table 2.2 shows the life expectancy for males and females who have reached a given age. These results represent the averages for the Australian population and use the 2000/02 census data. You can use this table to form an estimate of your own life expectancy if you apply a bit of common sense.

**Table 2.2: life expectancies**

| Age | Male | Female | Age | Male | Female |
|---|---|---|---|---|---|
| 50 | 30.39 | 34.51 | 73 | 12.11 | 14.78 |
| 51 | 29.49 | 33.58 | 74 | 11.50 | 14.05 |
| 52 | 28.59 | 32.66 | 75 | 10.90 | 13.33 |
| 53 | 27.69 | 31.73 | 76 | 10.32 | 12.63 |
| 54 | 26.80 | 30.82 | 77 | 9.77 | 11.94 |
| 55 | 25.92 | 29.91 | 78 | 9.24 | 11.27 |
| 56 | 25.05 | 29.00 | 79 | 8.73 | 10.61 |
| 57 | 24.19 | 28.10 | 80 | 8.24 | 9.98 |
| 58 | 23.34 | 27.21 | 81 | 7.77 | 9.38 |
| 59 | 22.49 | 26.32 | 82 | 7.32 | 8.81 |
| 60 | 21.66 | 25.44 | 83 | 6.89 | 8.27 |
| 61 | 20.84 | 24.57 | 84 | 6.48 | 7.76 |
| 62 | 20.04 | 23.71 | 85 | 6.11 | 7.28 |
| 63 | 19.24 | 22.85 | 86 | 5.77 | 6.83 |
| 64 | 18.46 | 22.00 | 87 | 5.47 | 6.41 |
| 65 | 17.70 | 21.15 | 88 | 5.20 | 6.02 |
| 66 | 16.95 | 20.32 | 89 | 4.95 | 5.66 |
| 67 | 16.21 | 19.49 | 90 | 4.74 | 5.33 |
| 68 | 15.48 | 18.67 | 91 | 4.54 | 5.03 |
| 69 | 14.78 | 17.87 | 92 | 4.36 | 4.75 |
| 70 | 14.08 | 17.08 | 93 | 4.19 | 4.50 |
| 71 | 13.41 | 16.29 | 94 | 4.03 | 4.28 |
| 72 | 12.75 | 15.53 | 95 | 3.87 | 4.07 |

*Source*: Australian life tables 2000/02

First we should recognise that this will not be a comfortable exercise. There are few things that are less comfortable than trying to realistically predict how much time we have left. That said, it is useful and necessary in order to understand whether you are on track to live out your remaining years in comfort or whether some serious changes need to be made.

Start by using the table to find the life expectancy for someone of your gender and current age; for example, a male currently aged 75 has a life expectancy of 11 years. Then apply an adjustment to this number that reflects your own sense of general wellbeing, fitness and use of life-shortening substances. If you are a fit 75-year-old male who has an active life who doesn't smoke or drink to excess then you might want to add five years to the average life expectancy. If you do not live like this then you might realistically hope for, say, 10 years or less depending on your circumstances. The important thing is to be realistic.

## When will you retire?

To a certain degree, the interaction of how much money you will need in retirement and when you start to need it are the big parameters that you can play with in terms of generating a successful retirement strategy. If you want a lifestyle that is significantly more expensive than your current lifestyle, and you want it to start when you are 50 rather than in your 60s, then you may be in trouble—or at least you may have some reality road bumps headed your way.

In addition, you may decide that you will want to work part time for at least some part of your retirement. Transitioning slowly between full-time work and retirement can have a number of benefits not just in relation to your income needs. It can help you and your family manage the change from work to retirement, and it may help your employer or business by maintaining access to your experience.

The age at which you retire is not set in stone. While we think of age 65 as being the general retirement age, the reality is that for many people it will be different to this. The Age Pension is currently available for males who are over

65 and for females who are over 63, but these starting ages are proposed to change to age 67 for people born after 1 January 1957. Our actual retirement age will depend on our own circumstances, but for consistency with the notional view that people retire at 65 we use this age for many of the case studies in this book.

## Where are you now?

Now that you have a broad sense of where you want to go and how long you have to get there, you need to spend some time thinking about the start of the journey. Where are you now? Do you properly understand your current situation — your launching point for the future?

Getting a good picture of your current situation involves understanding what your current resources are. This will include your major assets and liabilities and it will also include your earning potential.

### Assets

Your major assets are things like the primary residence, investment properties, your superannuation balance and any other investments you may have. It may also include your own business, but you need to be realistic about what it would be worth if you weren't working in it.

### Liabilities

The major liabilities are simply the debts you have on these assets, plus any other long-term debt that you may have. You should pay particular attention to the other debt because long-term debt without a corresponding asset indicates a problem. Whether it is a credit card, personal finance or a tax scheme or business gone bad, the problem needs to be recognised and dealt with.

### Earning potential

Earning potential is hard to estimate with accuracy, however if you are a long way from retirement you don't need to be hugely accurate. If you think you can realistically (and actually want to) do your boss's job or boss's boss's job then have a stab at what you think this person might be paid and how long it will take to get there. You also need to take into account your partner's income and whether there will be periods of time when one or both of you will not be earning income, for example to raise children.

The important part of this is identifying any periods of your working life where there is going to be surplus income and then having a plan for investing that surplus income.

## Where is your superannuation?

At first glance, understanding where your superannuation is seems likely a pretty basic thing to know, but you would be surprised how many people are unsure about where it is and even how many superannuation accounts they have.

During 2008, *Choice* magazine commissioned a report by a leading superannuation consultancy, Rice Warner, on the number of superannuation accounts that we have in Australia. The report found that there were over 13 million additional and probably unnecessary superannuation accounts. This included an estimated 6.4 million lost superannuation accounts containing almost $13 billion in total. These are superannuation accounts where the fund administrator no longer knows the address details of the owner of the account.

These unnecessary accounts highlight several problems. Additional accounts will usually mean that people are paying more fees than they need to. It will also be harder for the owners of these multiple accounts to keep track of their accounts and to implement consistent investment strategies. The number of lost accounts is even more worrying, because they indicate a real risk that some of this money will never be claimed by its rightful owners.

So the first thing to do is to make sure you know where all of your superannuation accounts are. If you are not sure, start by making a list of each employer you have had since 1992 as this was the year that compulsory super started.

Next you need to confirm that you know where the superannuation contributions were made by each of those employers. If you are not sure, there is a good online service called the SuperSeeker offered by the Australian Taxation Office: <https://superseeker.super.ato.gov.au/individuals/default.aspx?pid=0>.

## How much risk can you handle?

There is an important definitional aspect to 'risk' here. In the superannuation world 'risk' is not the chance of losing all of your money, rather it is a measure of volatility — the movement up and down in the value of the investment.

Don't think of 'risk' in the same way that you do with, say, a bet on a horse. In that situation the risk is clearly one of losing all of your money. As a general rule, superannuation fund investment options don't include options where you could lose everything. That said, some superannuation funds now offer the ability to invest in the shares of a single company; however, the trustees of those superannuation funds usually have controls in place to stop investors putting all of their superannuation into the shares of a single company.

Nonetheless, you still need to be aware of your own sense of preparedness and comfort to take on volatility.

Most superannuation funds offer you investment choices that will allow you to tailor how much risk or volatility your superannuation fund will experience. These choices range from a cash-style option which should experience very little volatility through to investment options that are close to 100 per cent shares, with lots of options that are in between. The trade-off here is that the cash option will almost certainly produce the lowest average investment return over the long term.

Again, your investment goals and time frames play a part in determining how much risk you should take on. If your investment goal is to get an investment return of at least 3 per cent per annum more than inflation (after fees and tax) over a time frame of more than 10 years, then you could argue that cash has the least chance of achieving this goal. A balanced investment option with around 60 per cent shares would have a much higher chance of achieving this goal. You could therefore argue that investing in cash to achieve this goal over this time frame is actually the riskiest approach to take, as it has the lowest chance of success.

No matter how good your understanding of the issues and how sound your strategy may be, if you embark on an investment strategy that has you fully invested in shares when you know that this will keep you awake at night worrying, that investment strategy may not be right for you.

Your superannuation fund provider may provide you with a risk-profiling tool that will help you understand your own tolerance for risk. BT Financial Group has a good one and it is available through its website at <www.bt.com.au/investors>.

## It's not just about you

For many of us, planning for our retirement is something that needs to be done not just in respect of ourselves but for our partner or spouse, and in some cases for other financial dependants, as well. While understanding the costs associated with the lifestyle requirements of both of you is one part, making sure that you have taken into account your partner's superannuation position is also important.

Many of the things we have just covered will need to be done with your partner in mind — not just his or her life expectancy, but also risk appetite, plans around when to retire from the workforce and how retirement will be spent.

Equally, if you have parents with limited retirement resources, or other financial dependants, will you need to allow for their needs during your own retirement years?

## Help is available

Throughout this book, you will see reference to the FIDO superannuation and pension calculators (available at <www.fido.gov.au>) as these calculators provide good, easy-to-use tools that will help you see the impacts that the various strategies can have on your retirement outcomes. This is a service provided by the Australian Securities & Investments Commission.

The basic information you need to get going is:

- ⇨ your current age
- ⇨ your current salary
- ⇨ your current superannuation account balance
- ⇨ your current superannuation fee structure
- ⇨ your planned retirement age.

Most superannuation funds now provide comprehensive self-help education services on their websites. These sites not only give you access to your own details but also the ability to make online changes to how your superannuation fund is being managed. In addition, they often provide calculators and tools to help you with this process.

Many members of corporate funds, and employees of larger employers using industry funds and employer master trusts, can also benefit from education seminars that are run at the workplace. These are a great way to learn more about your own superannuation arrangements and, importantly, to find out what sort of options and choices you have with your superannuation fund. If you have access to these seminars, make the most of it and go along. Ultimately it is a service that you are probably paying for.

## Where to from here?

By now you should at least have a sense of your starting position and resources. You should also have a view of your end goal and your time frames for both before and after retirement. You should also now be thinking about how well you can cope with the ups and downs that your investments will go through along the way.

If you go back to the holiday analogy, you can see that an important first step to your holiday plan has happened. You know where you are now, you have an idea of where you want to go, who you want to go with and how long you have to get there. You also have a sense of whether you want to have a nice smooth ride even if it takes longer, or whether you are prepared to go a bumpier route in order to get there a bit quicker.

A successful strategy is one that takes all of these building blocks into account without ignoring the fact that the only thing you can know for certain about the future is that the future is not known.

The next four chapters will help you do some more serious holiday planning. They also outline some strategies that will help you get much more out of your super. Some of the strategies cost virtually nothing to implement. Some strategies require a bit more effort and some sacrifice in terms of current spending patterns.

These chapters are split depending upon your current age and more specifically on how long you have to go before your retirement commences. While some of the strategies are specific to each age profile, it is worth reading all of the chapters to get a sense of the big levers — the ones that don't change based on your age — and to get a sense of some of the things that you may need to do if your planned retirement age varies significantly from age 65. If you are 65 now and plan to work for 10 more years then you will benefit from reading both chapter 5 and 6. If you are 30 now and plan to retire when you are 50, then you will benefit from reading all of the chapters.

*Where to from here — in your 20s and 30s . . . turn to page 29.*

*Where to from here — from 40 to 55 . . . turn to page 55.*

*Where to from here—from 55 to retirement . . . turn to page 87.*

*Where to from here—in retirement and beyond . . . turn to page 119.*

# Chapter 3

## Where to from here — in your 20s or 30s

Let's acknowledge that thinking about retirement is not something that most 20 and 30 year olds will do every day. Let's be honest and say it is something that they won't normally think about at all. Herein lies the great irony for this age bracket, because once you are old enough to think about retirement often, you will be wishing that you thought about it just once when you were in your 20s.

The other great irony for readers in this age bracket is that you may be thinking that you don't actually have much superannuation to salvage. While the investment markets tanked in 2008, if you didn't actually have that much invested in 2007 then the impact on your account balance wasn't huge.

So if you don't think about superannuation, and you don't have much superannuation to worry about salvaging, why should you read this book? The reason is that for you the underlying message of this book is not *salvaging super*, but rather it is about understanding and taking advantage of an opportunity that may generate a lotto-like prize — without a significant element of chance. For someone who doesn't have a large amount of invested assets, the collapse of financial markets in 2008 has offered a once-in-a-generation opportunity to start some serious investing at a time when share prices are relatively cheap.

If you are lucky enough, and smart enough, to take an interest in your superannuation at this stage of your life, the first thing you should do is give yourself a large pat on the back. If you have been given this book by a parent or older friend then still pat yourself on the back for reading this far. When you finish the book and get your superannuation on track then remember to thank the person who got you going on this route. By starting this process earlier in your life, you will either save a small fortune or dramatically increase your lifestyle in retirement.

In the earlier chapters you will have seen that to secure financial independence in retirement you need to understand your starting position and your end goals and time frames. You will have developed a sense of whether you are prepared to take on volatility of returns in order to achieve those goals with more certainty and speed or whether you will be more comfortable taking longer to get there for a smoother ride. You will have an understanding of how much money you will need to make your retirement financially secure.

The biggest and best resource that you have going for you is time. We have already seen that time is one of the four key things that can make a difference to your superannuation and ultimately how well you will live in retirement.

Given your age, you will have the benefit of compulsory superannuation contributions being made to a superannuation account in your name for most of your working life, as this current system of compulsory superannuation started in 1992. Despite this, there is a high probability that you will have only a marginal retirement outcome on your current path.

Assuming that you will work for 40 years (from age 25 to 65) and make no decisions about your superannuation other than to keep tabs on where it is, your superannuation may be sufficient to maintain a post-retirement income of less than 50 per cent of your pre-retirement income. Can you imagine comfortably living on half of your current salary? What could you afford? More importantly, what couldn't you afford? This result would almost certainly mean a reduced standard of living in retirement.

By doing a few little things early on in your working life, you can generate some significant improvements on this outcome.

## Understand the journey

Before we launch into strategies, you should revisit the journey you are trying to make. This means making sure that you know where you are starting from, where you are trying to get to and how long you can take to get there. As with any journey, it is often important to make the most of the travel rather than making the destination the single important element.

Any process of saving or investing for the future must by definition have an element of present-day sacrifice. If you don't do this early in your working life, the amount you will have to save out of future income will need to be larger—and the longer you leave it the bigger the sacrifices will become.

Given the long time frames involved, it is also important to keep in mind that the end result is about lifestyle, not a specific dollar amount. We use dollars as a means of quantifying the cost of the desired lifestyle, and we do this by converting the superannuation account balance at retirement into a post-retirement income. The methodology for the conversion is complicated and takes into account many assumptions about how long you are expected to live, the investment returns on your superannuation balance while in retirement, and cost of living increases.

As a way of trying to get a handle on lifestyle results, we try to understand the difference between pre-retirement salary and post-retirement salary. If your lifestyle immediately prior to retirement costs $50 000 a year in today's after-tax dollars, maintenance of that lifestyle after retirement is going to cost a similar amount. There are some aspects of retired life that are less costly compared to pre-retirement, such as travel to work, clothing and fast food. In addition, there are tax breaks on income you receive once you are retired which mean that you don't have to earn as much to maintain the same level of after-tax income. That said, there may be other expense lines that increase in retirement, such as travel, hobbies and health care.

We can therefore reflect the success (or otherwise) of these strategies by showing the post-retirement salary as a percentage of your pre-retirement salary. Any strategy that delivers a post-retirement salary result of better than 70 per cent of pre-retirement salary is generally going to be worth a look.

## Strategy 1: consolidation and fee management

By now you should have a handle on all of your superannuation accounts. The next step is to think about getting all of the superannuation accounts transferred into the one fund. This is called 'consolidation', and the fund you choose will be able to help you organise this. This is especially important to do when you are young. In the following strategies you will see that little positive changes over a long time frame can make a big positive difference to the end result. However, time and compound interest work just as well in the opposite direction if you are paying more fees than necessary.

A simple comparison using the FIDO superannuation calculator shows that splitting your superannuation across one good low-cost superannuation fund and one average-cost retail superannuation fund over 35 years of your working life can reduce your end balance by $24 000 if you are earning $50 000 per annum. This in turn reduces your superannuation balance at 65 by nearly 8 per cent. This doesn't sound like that much, but remember that for someone who doesn't consolidate superannuation, having only two superannuation accounts is going to be the best-case scenario. The reality is that people who don't consolidate superannuation could wind up with one superannuation account for every job they have had. How many jobs have you had since 1992?

The FIDO superannuation calculator also allows you to play around with different fee structures, and it is very important to correctly understand your own fees before using the calculator. Your annual superannuation statement should (by law) itemise and explain all of the fees that apply to your account. One trick with the FIDO calculator is to remember that management costs include underlying investment management fees and any other fees based on account balance.

As a guide, large industry and corporate funds as well as large employers within an employer super master trust may be charging less than 1 per cent of the assets for these fees, while retail funds may be as high as 2 per cent of the assets. Remember that the retail fund management cost may include an adviser service fee so it is important to separate that fee and not double-count it when using the calculator. If your annual statement does indicate that you have an adviser service fee, make sure that you are getting what you pay for — advice may actually be a great thing to explore.

There are three important things to do before you consolidate superannuation accounts.

Check whether there are any termination or exit penalties with each fund that you wish to transfer out of. Most funds will charge you a processing fee of up to $100 to do the transfer. The benefits of not paying multiple administration fees usually make consolidation worthwhile even if a termination fee has to be paid. Even large industry funds — usually some of the cheapest funds available — will charge you around $80 a year as a base administration charge on your superannuation account, so you can see that you will be able to recoup the termination charge relatively quickly.

Your preferred superannuation fund may be different to any of your existing funds. There are a number of different types of superannuation funds and they can offer a variety of services and cost structures. The range of cost structures and benefits is quite broad, so you need to do some homework on this. There are now a few reasonable websites that can help you choose a good superannuation fund, and one of the better ones is Applecheck at <www.chantwest.com.au>. This service allows you to compare funds in terms of both fees and services.

An important thing to remember when comparing superannuation funds is the cost of insurance. This can vary a lot between funds to the point that the insurance differences can outweigh the administration fee differences, especially if you have a large amount of life insurance cover. It is therefore important to have in mind the amount of life insurance cover you need — as opposed to the amount of cover you currently have — when you are making your fund comparisons.

Transferring your superannuation account balance from one fund to another is relatively easy (though harder than transferring money from one bank to another), but there may be real issues in transferring your life insurance from one fund to another.

In many cases, you will need to reapply for your life insurance cover in the new fund. This may mean that you will have to complete medical questionnaires and may even need to have a medical examination with a doctor. If your health has deteriorated since getting cover in your old fund, you may not be able to get the same or an appropriate level of cover in the new fund. It is therefore very important to get your insurance cover set up in your new fund before you cancel your cover in the old fund.

If it turns out to be too difficult to transfer your insurance arrangements, or if one of your old funds has very good insurance that can't be matched in your new preferred superannuation fund, consider leaving those insurance arrangements in place with a nominal amount of your superannuation in the fund to cover the cost of the insurance premiums. You will need to take this extra superannuation fund into account when dealing with other aspects of your superannuation strategy, however the inconvenience of two funds compared to one may be worthwhile for the sake of the better insurance arrangements.

There are other benefits of consolidation. Once your funds are consolidated, it is much easier to implement the other strategies you will see here. In addition, it reduces the risk that you will lose track of one of your superannuation accounts in the future. Since compulsory superannuation was introduced in 1992, Australians have lost track of over six million superannuation accounts with nearly $13 billion in them as at 2008. That is one lost account for every two working Australians.

The other thing to remember is that in most cases you no longer need to use the superannuation fund that your employer uses. You now have the right to direct your employer contributions into a superannuation fund of your choice. This means that once you have been through the process of consolidating your superannuation arrangements you can ask your employer to make future contributions to that fund and you won't need to consolidate your superannuation every time you change jobs.

## Strategy 2: choose your investment option

As you are at the early stages of your super accumulation stage, choosing the right way to have your superannuation invested, when coupled with a long time frame, can make a very substantial difference to your final superannuation balance.

Almost all superannuation funds offer you investment choice within that fund. Interestingly, superannuation fund trustees — the people who are ultimately responsible for the sound management and compliance of funds — must allow for the fact that some members will not actually make a choice. As a result, each superannuation fund has what is called a 'default investment option'. This is the investment option that your contributions will be invested in until you advise the trustee that you want to use something else.

Most funds will segment their investment options into one of six or so categories based on a risk versus return profile:

- *Cash:* 100 per cent invested in cash or similar securities.
- *Conservative:* Approximately 30 per cent invested in growth-style investments (Australian shares, international shares and property) and 70 per cent invested in income-style investments (cash, Australian fixed interest or bonds and international fixed interest).
- *Moderately conservative:* Approximately 50 per cent invested in growth-style investments and 50 per cent invested in income-style investments.

- ⇨ *Balanced:* Approximately 70 per cent invested in growth-style investments and 30 per cent invested in income-style investments.
- ⇨ *Growth:* Approximately 85 per cent invested in growth-style investments and 15 per cent invested in income-style investments.
- ⇨ *High growth:* Approximately 95 per cent invested in growth-style investments. Some small amounts of cash may exist as a result of cash flow requirements.

Funds differ in how they describe their options. Some funds will call 50 per cent growth/50 per cent income a balanced option, while other funds will call 70 per cent growth/30 per cent income a balanced option. The important thing is the amount of growth assets (shares or property) versus the amount of income or defensive assets (fixed interest and cash), rather than the name of the investment option. I have used the asset allocations shown above for all projections in this book.

The cash option will offer a low long-term return with low volatility (or risk). In contrast, the high-growth option will generally achieve the highest long-term return, however it will have higher volatility over shorter periods. The other options fall in between in terms of both return and volatility.

There is an important thing to note here and that is the word 'generally'. You can show data that reveals over a specific 10-year period some of the more conservative options outperform the high-growth options—the 10 years between 1 January 1999 and 31 December 2008 for example.

*Generally* the more growth assets your investments contain, the higher return you will receive over the long term. For projections we need to use an estimate of investment performance in the future. The projections used in our case studies use estimated future investment performance supplied by ASIC (as shown in table 3.1.).

**Table 3.1: estimated future investment performance**

| Investment option | Estimate of future long-term (10+ years) investment performance before tax and fees |
|---|---|
| High-growth option (95% growth assets) | 9.0% pa |
| Growth option (85% growth assets) | 8.5% pa |
| Balanced option (70% growth assets) | 8.0% pa |
| Conservative option (35% growth assets) | 6.0% pa |
| Capital stable or cash (0% growth assets) | 5.5% pa |

*Source:* FIDO and Chant West.

Most funds offer you not only a choice of investments around a risk and return profile, but also a choice of different fund managers and even individual company securities. The important part of this is to realise that the choice you make here can make a very substantial difference to the end result you generate.

## Balanced option

The balanced option is often the default investment option that is used where you make no active investment option decision.

Tom is a 25 year old with no existing superannuation account balance, on an income of $50 000 a year and invested in a balanced investment option, making no additional contributions. Using the FIDO superannuation calculator you will see that Tom will generate a superannuation account balance of $311 000 (in today's dollars) by the time he gets to age 65.

The $50 000 salary is clearly just an example. The FIDO calculator uses one salary level and indexes that salary for inflation only. The reality of course is that people will have different pay outcomes throughout their working life. The important thing here is not how close or far the $50 000 is from reality, but rather the extent of difference the post-retirement salary is to the pre-retirement salary.

It is worth remembering that someone earning $50 000 a year pays around $9000 a year in tax, and therefore this salary equates to a $41 000 after-tax income. As at early 2009, you don't pay any tax on income derived from allocated or term pensions — so $41 000 pa is the level of pay we need to target to maintain Tom's income after retirement.

The FIDO pension calculator shows that if Tom invested this $311 000 when he was 65 into a term allocated pension for the same term as his life expectancy he would receive a pension income of about $24 200 a year — or 59 per cent of his pre-retirement income. Not a great result, and one that would almost certainly cause a reduction in his lifestyle. A term allocated pension is a retirement product that will pay out a reasonably stable income over a target time period. Using the life expectancy table on page 19 you can see that a male aged 65 at 2008 has a life expectancy of 17.7 years, so using a term of 18 years in a term allocated pension calculator is a good guide to working out how much income a male will have in retirement if he retires at 65. A female's life expectancy at the same point is 21.2 years and her post-retirement income would be about $21 000 a year or 51 per cent of pre-retirement income.

## Cash option

If Tom had invested in the cash option rather than balanced over the full 40 years of his working life, his superannuation benefit would most likely be around $187 000, or around two-thirds of the result using the balanced option. The resulting post-retirement income can only be described as very poor.

## High-growth option

On the other hand, if Tom decided to use a high-growth investment option over the full 40 years of his working life, he would produce a superannuation benefit of around $386 000, or $75 000 more than if he had left the money in the default balanced option. That extra money takes the post-retirement salary up to $29 900 on average, or 73 per cent of his pre-retirement income.

Not a single extra cent of contribution is required to generate this extra money. No reduction of current lifestyle. No additional saving or sacrifice. If you are in your 20s the best investment strategy for retirement is simply to take the time to read this chapter, call or log on to your superannuation fund's website and fill in a form to make an investment change to a high-growth option and then relax with the knowledge that your superannuation is now invested in a way that will generate a better long-term investment return. You might be concerned that there is higher risk with this approach, but remember that having time up your sleeve changes the way we look at risk.

## Strategy 3: make small regular additional contributions

If you want to do even more for your superannuation, a small $20 a week additional contribution made from after-tax salary for the full 40 years before retiring (all invested in a high-growth investment option) will produce a superannuation account balance of around $524 000 by age 65. This is an extra $138 000 in today's dollars. The resulting average post-retirement salary for a male is around $40 600, or 99 per cent of pre-retirement salary. Again that is in today's dollars.

If you seriously can't afford to find $20 a week to take advantage of this then do something drastic like asking your parents to think about helping you make the necessary contributions until you can afford to take it on yourself.

### Co-contributions

One of the reasons that this strategy is so powerful is that it takes advantage of the federal government co-contribution scheme. If you earn less than $60 342 in the 2008/09 year and you make an after-tax contribution, the government will also make a contribution to your superannuation account. If you earn less than $30 342 in the 2008/09 year, the government will contribute $1.50 for every extra dollar that you put in up to a maximum co-contribution of $1500 a year. The amount of money that the government contributes for you reduces as you earn more money above the $30 342 threshold, and cuts out completely once you earn more than $60 342 per annum. These salary thresholds are indexed each year at 30 June.

This strategy is one of those absolute 'no brainers' that you get to hear about every now and then. In effect, the government will give you money, simply because you save a little bit for your own future — what a great scheme! As a result of the 2009 Federal Budget, this maximum co-contribution rate will temporarily reduce for the five years between 1 July 2009 to 30 June 2014, but this temporary reduction doesn't make a significant difference to the end result and it is still a great benefit.

You don't have to apply for these government contributions, either. If you make after-tax contributions to your superannuation, the fund will report those contributions to the Tax Office and the government will then make the co-contribution directly into your superannuation fund for you.

The only crazy thing here is the number of Australians that don't use it.

## Pre-tax contributions

If you earn more than the co-contribution cut-off salary ($60 342 per annum in the 2008/09 year), the strategy of making extra contributions still holds. With a higher salary, though, you may be better off making your additional regular contributions through a pre-tax arrangement or salary sacrifice. This simply means that you direct some of your pre-tax income into your superannuation fund. This income then gets taxed at the superannuation tax rate, which is lower than your marginal tax rate.

The reason that pre-tax contributions work for higher paid people comes back to the differences in tax for individuals compared to superannuation funds. If you earned $70 000 for example and were thinking about contributing $1000 a year (around $20 a week) into your superannuation fund, how much tax would you save?

That final $1000 of salary that you receive for the year is taxed (in the 2008/09 tax year) at 30¢ in the dollar or by 30 per cent. By receiving this money as income you pay $300 in income tax. If you invest the remaining $700 you would then pay a further 30 per cent of the investment earnings as income tax.

If that final $1000 of pay had been directed into your superannuation fund pre-tax, the entire $1000 goes into your superannuation fund. The fund then pays $150 (15 per cent) contributions tax, leaving $850 to be invested into your superannuation fund account. The earnings on that $850 are taxed at a maximum rate of 15 per cent — not 30 per cent if this was held outside of superannuation.

The tax benefits for pre-tax contributions go up as your marginal income tax rate increases — the more tax you pay the more tax you can save by using pre-tax contributions.

The cut-off point for whether you are better off making pre-tax contributions or post-tax contributions to your superannuation fund is dependent on your particular circumstances, but as a general rule if your salary is more than the co-contribution cut-off level then you should be looking at pre-tax contributions.

To start making pre-tax contributions, you should talk to your employer's payroll person and ask for help to set up a regular contribution out of your pre-tax pay.

## Strategy 4: get more out of your superannuation

The strategies that we have looked at so far are all about how to better grow your superannuation account. There are a few other things that you can do to get more out of your superannuation.

### Insurance

Life insurance is another element of superannuation funds that can really make a difference to how much value you get from your fund. As a general rule, most working Australians should take out their life insurance through their superannuation fund. In fact, it is fair to say that if you have a personal life insurance policy as well as a separate superannuation fund, you may very well be throwing money away.

Life insurance premiums are tax deductible to the superannuation fund, and most will either pass the tax deduction on to members or take it into account when setting premiums for their members. The premiums for personal life insurance policies are generally not tax deductible to a PAYG taxpayer. If your marginal income tax rate is higher than 15 per cent (if you earn more than $34 000 per annum for the 2008/09 tax year), you could get an immediate tax benefit by having your life insurance in your superannuation fund.

*But wait, there's more!*

Superannuation funds can generally buy insurance in a wholesale market and at group rates. The underlying cost of the insurance can therefore be cheaper than if you approached an insurance company directly. In addition, the premiums effectively come out of your superannuation contributions, so the cost of the premiums doesn't have to be covered by your net pay. That doesn't mean that it's free — obviously the insurance premiums paid out reduce the end superannuation benefit, but if you have life insurance then the net cost to you will almost certainly be less if you run it through your superannuation fund.

The combination of all of these elements means that those on the top marginal tax rate may be able to save between 40 per cent and 60 per cent of the net cost of life insurance premiums if they move their insurance into their superannuation fund.

Remember that when comparing fees and services between superannuation funds you also need to compare the cost of life insurance between superannuation funds. Quite often the differences in premiums charged for life insurance can vary more than the difference in administration fees.

If you have a big mortgage and dependants then you probably need between seven and 10 times your annual pay to be properly covered. The cost of this level of cover can be in the thousands of dollars a year, so these savings can be significant. It is therefore worth spending some time here on how much insurance you should have.

There are a lot of websites offering help on how much life insurance you should have. You do need to exert some care with these sites as they are often provided by either insurance companies or by insurance broking or advice businesses, and therefore there may be some benefits to these organisations in encouraging high levels of cover. That said, Australians are generally considered to be underinsured in terms of life insurance.

Your superannuation fund may have come with a default level of insurance cover. This is a level of cover that you receive automatically when you join the fund. While this is a helpful start, these default levels of cover are generally less than the true insurance needs that you may have. Your superannuation fund may offer a self-help calculator to assist with this.

The better websites will generally ask you to put in more details, as the more details you put in the more the answer is tailored to your situation. The good ones also help you understand what it is you are trying to cover. One of these better ones is on the BT Financial Group website <www.bt.com.au/investors/>.

The starting position for working it out yourself is to try to determine the impact on your family or partner if you were to die. This needs to take into account not only the loss of your existing and future income, but also any existing mortgages or debts that become difficult to pay if you were to die. It is not just about employed partners either. If one of you is not employed, but is bringing up children for example, you should also consider the cost of child care and home maintenance if that partner were to die.

If you don't have dependants or a partner, your life insurance needs may be considerably less.

## Education

Most superannuation funds now provide comprehensive self-help education services on their websites. These sites not only give you access to your own details but also the ability to make online changes to how your superannuation fund is being managed. In addition, they often provide calculators and tools to help you with this process.

Many members of corporate funds and employees of larger employers using industry funds and employer master trusts can also benefit from education seminars that are run at the workplace. These are a great way to learn more about your own superannuation arrangements and, importantly, to find out what sort of options and choices you have with your superannuation fund. If you have access to these seminars, make the most of it and go along. Ultimately it is a service that you are probably paying for.

## Advice

No matter how good the websites, calculators, written communication material and education seminars, personalised advice should be better. If the advice is coming from a qualified expert, with your best interests at heart, then there is no better way to get your own situation and needs fully explained and solutions explored. You can access financial advice through most superannuation funds these days, including industry funds.

If you are in a retail fund or part of a small employer group within an employer master trust then there is a good chance that you may be charged an adviser service fee each year. This will be shown on your annual statement if it is the case, along with contact details for your adviser. If you are being charged such a fee, it may be worthwhile talking to the adviser about your own situation and what sort of help he or she can provide you with for the service fee and how much extra it would cost to get more comprehensive advice.

Do your research though and ensure that if you do decide to get additional advice it is from someone appropriately qualified, and that the advice won't be conflicted via commissions received for recommending certain products.

We cover the issues of how to get advice the right way in chapter 7.

One of the other important aspects that an adviser can assist with is the implementation of your strategies. For some people, a difficult final step after doing the research and working out the best course of action to follow is the actual execution of the strategy. The very fact that you have gone to the trouble and expense of getting financial advice will help you follow through and implement that advice.

## Strategy 5: plan to deal with periods of no contributions

As you are in your 20s or 30s, there may come a time when you (or your partner) will not be able to work for a few years, especially if you have children. In fact, if you are in your 20s now, you could argue that it is almost certain that you or your current or future partner will experience either a period outside the paid workforce or a period where there is only one income coming into the household. The cause — whether it is for raising children, being between jobs, being single or divorced, or something worse like ill health or injury — is largely irrelevant in terms of understanding and dealing with the implications for your retirement. The critical thing is to acknowledge that there is a high probability that a period without two incomes will occur and to do some planning that allows for this situation.

The best strategy for dealing with this is to expect that this will happen at some point and to acknowledge that during these periods superannuation contributions will most likely stop for the person not working. Getting your superannuation ahead of the game during the periods of plenty is a logical and viable approach to dealing with this.

For most of us, planning our lives is an enjoyable exercise—even if the reality bears little resemblance to the plan. We generally enjoy thinking about how and where we are going to live, with whom, and whether we will have children or not. The suggestion here is to simply extend the planning process a little bit to include an awareness of the long-term future.

You would be surprised as to how much of a difference being out of the workforce for even a relatively short time can make. If we go back to the first superannuation account balance estimate we generated in this chapter, a full working life of 40 years produced a superannuation account balance at 65 of $311 000. If that person had started superannuation contributions at age 30 rather than 25, the account balance drops to $246 000—over 20 per cent lower.

You need to understand and plan for these periods of low-paid work or no work. By using the other strategies you can make up for these periods.

Additional contributions to the partner most likely to have a break from paid work can commence before the break starts, and in that way you can make up for the period where contributions won't be able to be made. Alternatively, these additional contributions can be saved outside of superannuation and then be contributed to that person's superannuation account once he or she ceases paid work, thereby allowing you to maximise the government co-contribution benefit.

Clearly there may be some periods without pay that can't be planned—especially as a result of illness or injury, or redundancy. The economic downturn that followed 2008 brought this home to many people around the world, and while this caused hardship for many people there is a fundamental lesson here around planning for the future. It is effectively a poor plan that relies on the assumption that the best outcome will always happen. In so many other parts of our lives, we realistically assess the upsides and downsides of a particular course of action. This can be within something as simple as driving through a red light because we are late, to insuring our house against the threat of fire.

And yet we rarely apply the same logic to long-range impacts of something that might be a virtual certainty, like reductions in family income due to periods where one partner may be out of paid work.

As you can see, each of these small changes applied over a long period of time can make a big difference. The trick is always the same: do it sooner rather than later.

## Summary of strategies

Table 3.2 (overleaf) summarises the value of all of the strategies we have looked at for someone with a $50 000 annual salary.

## Plan B

As with every good set of strategies, you should also consider whether there is an alternative way of achieving your goals. Let's try to find some other ways that you might be able to secure a comfortable retirement lifestyle, and then you can evaluate the probability of success and the potential pitfalls of adopting these strategies (see table 3.3, on page 53).

As you can see, you are actually blessed with access to the most powerful attribute of superannuation — the power of time. This element is the most powerful because it makes all of the strategies work harder for you.

**Table 3.2: strategy summary for 20s and 30s**

| | Strategy | Estimated lump sum | Estimated income or pension | Proportion of pre-retirement salary after tax ($41 000 pa) |
|---|---|---|---|---|
| 1 | Consolidate your superannuation into one primary account | Dependent on the number of accounts and costs of the various accounts you have | | |
| 2a | Do nothing — use a default balanced investment option | $311 000 at age 65 | $24 200 pa from age 65 | 59% |
| 2b | Change investments to cash and leave it there as a result of the 2008 sharemarket collapse | $187 000 at age 65 | $11 700 pa from age 65 | 29% |
| 2c | Change investments to high growth despite the 2008 sharemarket collapse | $386 000 at age 65 | $29 900 pa from age 65 | 73% |
| 2c & 3 | Make additional post-tax contributions of $1000 pa | $524 000 at age 65 | $40 600 pa from age 65 | 99% |
| 4 | Get more out of your superannuation | Your superannuation fund may offer you more services than you are using so check out the insurance, education and advice services available. | | |
| 5 | Deal with periods of low-paid work | For most Australian families there will be periods where one partner is out of work. Acknowledge that this is the most likely situation and plan accordingly. | | |

**Table 3.3: plan B strategies for 20s and 30s**

| Plan B strategy | Description | Risks and potential outcomes |
|---|---|---|
| Marry rich | You are good looking and plan to use this asset to secure the rich, successful (insert gender preference here) of your dreams. | Your potential partners get nervous when you refuse to sign the pre-nuptial agreements, and eventually you marry for love. Unfortunately, you are now 40 and have to fund your retirement out of the last half of your working life. |
| Die young | By dying before you reach retirement age you remove the need for financial security in retirement. | You decide later in life that dying isn't all that good an option and decide to live on — without the financial means to do so. |

It is a relatively simple thing for you to harness these strategies, and if you do so you will be able to easily and dramatically enhance your retirement lifestyle.

For the rest of us, it gets harder and harder.

## The next step

The action plan for you is relatively simple and it can be done in steps:

1 Consolidate — get your superannuation all in one good fund that suits you.

2 Choose your investment strategy — time is on your side and this allows you to look at risk differently.

3 Make a small additional regular contribution to your fund — a small amount now will save you needing to

make much bigger contributions later on, especially if you or your partner will spend some time out of the workforce in the future.

4 Use your fund's services — look at your life insurance needs, review the education services and think about getting financial advice.

Read the next chapter to see how to make the most of your big earning years — and some tips on what to do when you get ahead.

# Chapter 4

## Where to from here — from 40 to 55

For many of us in this age bracket, retirement is just starting to nudge our consciousness. It can still be thought of as far away, but equally it can be something that we can look forward to.

This period can be our most productive in terms of the money we will make. We will generally be getting into the most senior positions of our working life, or our business will hopefully now be well established and flourishing. As a result, this is the period where most people's income tends to be at its peak, or at least plateauing.

Equally, this can often be the period where our lifestyle costs are peaking. A combination of trying to pay off a mortgage, sending kids to school or university or having some more extravagant holidays can easily eat into that higher income.

It is also worth noting that people in this group generally have some superannuation already accumulated, and there is a very good chance that they will have seen their superannuation badly affected by the events of 2008. Once you have seen your superannuation account balance hit by something like the Global Financial Crisis, there is often a temptation to shift the remaining balance to a more conservative, 'safe' investment option such as cash. As you will see from the strategies outlined below, this could be one of the worst things you could do.

In the earlier chapters you will have seen that to secure financial independence in retirement, you need to understand your starting position and your end goals and time frames. You will have developed a sense of whether you are prepared to take on volatility of returns in order to achieve those goals with more certainty and speed, or whether you will be more comfortable taking longer to get there for a smoother ride. You will have an understanding of how much money you will need to make your retirement financially secure.

In this age bracket you have two main weapons to secure financial security. While the power of time is diminished somewhat compared to the people in their 20s and 30s, time can still be used to your advantage. The other main weapon will be to acknowledge and use your peaking earning capacity wisely.

For younger people in this age bracket — those close to 40 — you will have the benefit of compulsory superannuation contributions being made to a super account in your name for most of your working life — since 1992. Despite this, if you don't take an interest and make some key decisions with your superannuation, there is a high probability that you will have only a marginal retirement outcome.

For older people, the first 10 to 15 years of your working life may well have been without the benefit of superannuation. If this is the case you may well have a significant hole in your superannuation account balance and some serious work may be required to correct it.

Despite these potential problems, there are some strategies that you can use to generate some significant improvements to your financial security in retirement.

## Understand the journey

Before we launch into strategies, you should revisit the journey you are trying to make. This means making sure that you know where you are now, where you are trying to get to and how long you can take to get there. As with any journey, it is often important to make the most of the travel rather than making the destination the single important element.

Any process of saving or investing for the future must by definition have an element of present-day sacrifice. If you haven't done this early in your working life, the amount you will have to save out of current income will need to be larger—and the longer you leave it the bigger the sacrifices will become.

Given the long time frames involved, it is also important to keep in mind that the end result is about lifestyle, not a specific dollar amount. We use dollars as a means of quantifying the cost of the desired lifestyle, and we do this by converting the superannuation account balance at retirement into a post-retirement income. The methodology for the conversion is complicated and takes into account many assumptions about how long you are expected to live, the investment returns on your superannuation balance while in retirement, and cost of living increases.

As a way of trying to get a handle on lifestyle results, we try to understand the difference between pre-retirement and post-retirement salary. If your lifestyle immediately prior to retirement costs $80 000 a year in today's after-tax dollars, maintenance of that lifestyle after retirement is going to cost a similar amount. There are some aspects of retired life that are less costly compared to pre-retirement, such as travel to work, clothing and fast food. In addition, there are tax breaks on income you receive once you are retired which mean that you don't have to earn as much to maintain the same level of after-tax income. That said, there may be other expense lines that increase in retirement, such as travel, hobbies and health care.

We can therefore reflect the success (or otherwise) of these strategies by showing the post-retirement salary as a percentage of your pre-retirement salary. Any strategy that delivers a post-retirement salary result of better than 70 per cent of pre-retirement salary is generally going to be worth a look.

## Strategy 1: consolidation and fee management

We have seen that consolidating your super accounts is important because it helps you manage your fees and implement other strategies. This is especially important when you are in the middle of your career. In the earlier chapters we have seen that little positive changes over a long time frame can make a big positive difference to the end result. Time and compound interest work just as well in the opposite direction if you are paying higher fees than necessary.

Most employers you have had throughout your career so far have had to make superannuation contributions for you. If you haven't been an active participant in that process, your employer will have decided which superannuation fund they will use for your contributions. When you leave that employer they stop making contributions to that fund, and the fund then either maintains your account (while continuing to charge fees) or moves your account to another fund — which will then start charging fees on your account. If your account balance is very small, there is fee protection to stop your account being eaten up by fees, but these small accounts generally don't earn any interest either.

The full impact of all of this will depend on the number of accounts you accumulate, and the level of fees charged in your various inactive accounts. Someone who is currently 45, earning $150 000 per annum, and has four inactive super accounts with $20 000 in each account, would wind up with superannuation accounts totalling $431 000 at age 65. If this person consolidated those four inactive accounts at age 45, the total superannuation balance would be around $478 000, or 11 per cent or $47 000 more. The reduction in total value is simply a result of additional sets of fees. The numbers assume the same investment performance and contribution rate — fees are the only difference.

By the time you get to the middle stages of your working life, you may have had more than a dozen different jobs. The reality is that people who don't consolidate their superannuation could wind up with one superannuation account for every job they have had. How many jobs have you had since 1992?

The FIDO superannuation calculator (available at <www.fido.gov.au>) allows you to play around with different fee structures, and it is very important to correctly understand your own fees before using the calculator. Your annual superannuation statement should (by law) itemise and explain all of the fees that apply to your account.

One trick with the FIDO calculator is to remember that management costs include underlying investment management fees and any other fees based on account balance. Basically, everything that is charged to your account as a percentage of the assets is rolled up into this management cost. This will include things like investment management, some administration charges and any adviser service fees. It won't include dollar-per-week style administration charges, charges that are based on a percentage of the new contributions or insurance premiums.

As a guide, large industry and corporate funds as well as large employer groups within an employer superannuation master trust may be charging less than 1 per cent of the assets for these management costs, while retail funds may be as high as 2 per cent of the assets. Remember that the retail fund management cost may include an adviser service fee so it is important to separate that fee and not double-count it when using the calculator. If your annual statement does indicate that you have an adviser service fee, make sure that you are getting what you pay for — advice may actually be a great thing to explore.

An important thing to remember when comparing super funds is the cost of insurance. This can vary a lot between funds to the point that the insurance differences can outweigh the administration fee differences, especially if you have a large amount of life insurance cover. It is therefore important to have in mind the amount of life insurance cover you need — as opposed to the amount of cover you currently have — when you are making your fund comparisons. Transferring your superannuation account balance from one fund to another is relatively easy (though harder than transferring money from one bank to another), but there may be real issues in transferring your life insurance from one fund to another.

In many cases, you will need to reapply for your life insurance cover in the new fund. This may mean that you will have to complete medical questionnaires and may even need to have a medical examination with a doctor. If your health has deteriorated since getting cover in your old fund, you may not be able to get the same or an appropriate level of cover in the new fund. It is therefore very important to get your insurance cover set up in your new fund before you cancel your cover in the old fund.

If it turns out to be too difficult to transfer your insurance arrangements, or if one of your old funds has very good insurance that can't be matched in your new preferred super fund, consider leaving those insurance arrangements in place with a nominal amount of your superannuation in the fund to cover the cost of the insurance premiums. You will need to take this extra superannuation fund into account when dealing with other aspects of your superannuation strategy, however the inconvenience of two funds compared to one may be worthwhile for the sake of the better insurance arrangements.

There are other benefits of consolidation. Once your funds are consolidated, it is much easier to implement the other strategies here. In addition, it reduces the risk that you will lose track of one of your superannuation accounts in the future. Since compulsory superannuation was introduced in 1992, Australians have lost track of over six million superannuation accounts with nearly $13 billion in them as at 2008. That is one lost account for every two working Australians.

You no longer need to use the superannuation fund that your employer uses as the default arrangement. You now have the right to direct your employer contributions into a superannuation fund of your choice. This means that once you have been through the process of choosing a primary superannuation fund and consolidating your superannuation arrangements, you can ask your employer to make future contributions to that primary fund and you won't need to consolidate your superannuation every time you change jobs.

## Strategy 2: choose your investment option

After going through strategy 1, you will now have a good sense of the features of your fund. As part of this you will have noted that your fund has a selection of investment choices.

### A quick quiz

Without referring to your last set of superannuation statements, answer the following questions:

1 What type of investment option are your superannuation assets invested in?

2 What proportion of these investment options use growth assets?

3 Which fund managers are used to manage the options that you use?

If you haven't been able to answer all of these questions, think about how well you would have gone if these questions related to your banking arrangements or non-superannuation investments and then ask yourself, why the difference?

Most funds will segment their investment options into one of six or so categories based on a risk versus return profile:

- *Cash:* 100 per cent invested in cash or similar securities.
- *Conservative:* approximately 30 per cent invested in growth-style investments (Australian shares, international shares and property) and 70 per cent invested in income-style investments (cash, Australian fixed interest or bonds and international fixed interest).
- *Moderately conservative:* approximately 50 per cent invested in growth-style investments and 50 per cent invested in income-style investments.
- *Balanced:* approximately 70 per cent invested in growth-style investments and 30 per cent invested in income-style investments.
- *Growth:* approximately 85 per cent invested in growth-style investments and 15 per cent invested in income-style investments.
- *High growth:* approximately 95 per cent invested in growth-style investments. Some small amounts of cash may exist as a result of cash flow requirements.

Funds differ in how they describe their options. Some funds will call 50 per cent growth/50 per cent income a balanced option, while other funds will call 70 per cent growth/ 30 per cent income a balanced option. The important thing is the amount of growth assets (shares or property) versus the amount of income or defensive assets (fixed interest and cash), rather than the name of the investment option. I have used the asset allocations shown above for all projections in this book.

The cash option will offer a low long-term return with low volatility (or risk). In contrast, the high-growth option will generally achieve the highest long-term return, however it will have higher volatility over shorter periods. The other options fall in between in terms of both return and volatility.

There is an important thing to note here and that is the word 'generally'. You can show data that reveals over a specific 10-year period some of the more conservative options outperform the high-growth options — the 10 years between 1 January 1999 and 31 December 2008 for example.

*Generally* the more growth assets your investments contain, the higher return you will receive over the long term. For projections we need to use an estimate of investment performance in the future. The projections used in our case studies use estimated future investment performance supplied by ASIC (as shown in table 4.1.).

In addition, most funds offer you not only a choice of investments around a risk and return profile, but also different fund managers and even individual company securities.

The important part of this is to realise that the choice you make here can make a very substantial difference to the end result you generate.

**Table 4.1: estimated future investment performance**

| Investment option | Estimate of future long-term (10+ years) investment performance before tax and fees |
|---|---|
| High-growth option (95% growth assets) | 9.0% pa |
| Growth option (85% growth assets) | 8.5% pa |
| Balanced option (70% growth assets) | 8.0% pa |
| Conservative option (35% growth assets) | 6.0% pa |
| Capital stable or cash (0% growth assets) | 5.5% pa |

*Source:* FIDO and Chant West.

## Balanced option

Felicity is 50 years young with an existing superannuation balance of $150 000, and her salary is $100 000 a year. Her take-home or after-tax pay is $74 000 a year, based on the tax rates for the 2008/09 tax year.

She has made no active investment choice with her superannuation fund and her employer contributions are being invested in the default investment option, which is a balanced option. She is making no additional contributions, so the employer superannuation guarantee contributions — 9 per cent of her pay — are the only contributions being made.

Using the FIDO superannuation calculator you can see that Felicity will have an estimated superannuation account balance of $394 000 (in today's dollars) by the time she gets to age 65.

The FIDO pension calculator shows that if Felicity invests this $394 000 into a term allocated pension for the same term as her life expectancy she will receive a pension income of about $26 700 a year — or 36 per cent of her pre-retirement after-tax income. Not a great result, and one that would almost certainly cause a very significant reduction in Felicity's lifestyle.

A term allocated pension is a retirement product that will pay out a reasonably stable income over a target time period. A female aged 65 at 2008 has a life expectancy of 21.2 years, so using a term of 22 years in a term allocated pension calculator is a good guide to working out how much income a female will have in retirement if she retires at 65. A male's life expectancy at the same point is 17.7 years and the post-retirement income would be about $30 500 a year.

The $100 000 salary is clearly just an example. The FIDO calculator uses one salary level and indexes that salary for inflation only. The reality of course is that people will have different pay outcomes throughout their working life. The important thing here is not how close or far the $100 000 is from reality, but rather the extent of difference between the after-tax post-retirement pay and the pre-retirement pay.

## Cash option

If Felicity switches her superannuation into the cash option as a result of the 2008 sharemarket collapse rather than leave it in the balanced option over the remaining 15 years of her working life, her superannuation benefit would most likely be around $300 000. The lower expected return from the cash option could cost her nearly $100 000 of accumulated superannuation. The resulting post-retirement income can only be described as very poor.

## High-growth option

On the other hand, if Felicity switches to a high-growth investment option for the remaining 15 years of her working life, her superannuation benefit would most likely be around $439 000, or $45 000 more than if she had left the money in the balanced option. That extra money takes the post-retirement salary up to $29 700 on average, or 40 per cent of her pre-retirement income.

The thing to note here is that while switching to a high-growth option is helping, it is not going to fix the main problem that Felicity faces and that is a significant shortfall in retirement funding. In this situation she is going to have to apply a series of strategies to try to fix the problem — there is no single silver bullet. Getting the most out of the investment performance is going to be one of those important steps, and while you might be concerned that there is higher risk with this approach, you should remember that having time up your sleeve changes the way we look at risk.

While you may think that the example here is extreme, the statistics on the size of average superannuation accounts are scarily low. Table 4.2 shows the average member balance at 30 June 2008. These numbers are the consolidated member balances — not average account balances, which are even lower.

**Table 4.2: average member balances at 30 June 2008**

| Age group | Males | Females |
|---|---|---|
| 40 to 44 | $71 500 | $45 400 |
| 45 to 49 | $92 400 | $49 300 |

*Source:* Rice Warner Research.

The average member superannuation account balances are a consequence of both the number of years of contributions and the salaries of the members. In Felicity's case we have recognised that her current salary of $100 000 is nearly double the average salary in Australia and therefore we have assumed that her superannuation account balance would be double the average member balance for a female of her age.

Women generally have lower account balances than men of similar age. The combination of superannuation contributions not being made available for many women until the commencement of the superannuation guarantee in 1992, a higher proportion of women doing part-time work, and broken periods of paid employment to bring up children mean that many women on average have lower account balances. Unfortunately the problem is compounded because women have a longer life expectancy than men. This means that they need a larger superannuation account balance to maintain lifestyle, because women on average will live longer than men and therefore be retired for longer.

## Strategy 3: make regular additional contributions

Felicity has decided that while changing her investment strategy to a high-growth option will be worth doing, she clearly needs to do more in order to have a better retirement outcome than 40 per cent of her pre-retirement pay. She decides to make a regular monthly additional contribution of 6 per cent of her pre-tax salary for the remaining 15 years before retiring. This equates to about $500 per month of her pre-tax income in the first year, but it will go up in line with any salary increases in the future.

It is worth noting that, as this money is coming out of her pre-tax pay, it will be less than a 5 per cent reduction in her total after-tax pay. This is because the $6000 that she is contributing to superannuation would normally be taxed at her marginal income tax rate of 40 per cent rather than her average income tax rate of 26 per cent.

The FIDO superannuation calculator estimates that her superannuation account balance will now be around $546 000 at age 65, with an average post-retirement salary of $37 000 or 50 per cent of pre-retirement salary. Again that is in today's dollars.

This represents an additional $107 000 on top of that achieved by Felicity through strategy 2. Putting 6 per cent of her pre-tax pay into superannuation may be difficult, but we need to face up to the challenge that doing nothing will result in a very poor retirement outcome. The combination of strategies 2 and 3 have so far gained Felicity around $150 000 extra in her superannuation account, but her retirement lifestyle is going to be based on a post-retirement income of only 50 per cent of her pre-retirement income — she needs to find more.

## Co-contributions

If you earn less than $60 342 in the 2008/09 year, and you make an after-tax contribution, the government will also make a contribution to your superannuation account. If you earn less than $30 342 in the 2008/09 year, the government will contribute $1.50 for every extra dollar that you put in up to a maximum co-contribution of $1500 a year. The amount of money that the government contributes for you reduces as you earn more money above the $30 342 threshold, and cuts out completely once you earn more than $60 342 per annum. These salary thresholds are indexed each year at 30 June.

This strategy is one of those absolute 'no brainers' that you get to hear about every now and then. In effect, the government will give you money, simply because you save a little bit for your own future — what a great scheme!

As a result of the 2009 Federal Budget, this maximum co-contribution rate will temporarily reduce for the five years between 1 July 2009 to 30 June 2014, but this temporary reduction doesn't make a significant difference to the end result and it is still a great benefit.

You don't have to apply for these government contributions either. If you make after-tax contributions to your superannuation, the fund will report those contributions to the Tax Office and the government will then make the co-contribution directly into your superannuation fund for you.

The only crazy thing here is the number of Australians that don't use it.

As Felicity's salary is over the co-contribution salary threshold, she doesn't benefit from this scheme, but being on a higher tax bracket means that she can generate real tax savings by making her contributions pre-tax.

## Pre-tax or post-tax contributions

If you earn more than the co-contribution cut-off salary ($60 342 per annum in the 2008/09 year), the strategy of making extra contributions still holds. With a higher salary, though, you may be better off making your additional regular contributions through a pre-tax arrangement or salary sacrifice. This simply means that you direct some of your pre-tax income into your superannuation fund. This income then gets taxed at the superannuation tax rate, which is lower than your marginal tax rate.

In Felicity's case, her salary is $100 000 per annum, so her marginal rate is 40 per cent — every dollar that she earns over $75 000 is taxed by 40¢. The tax she pays on the last $6000 she earns in the year is $2400 (ignoring the Medicare levy). By diverting that $6000 into superannuation she loses only 15 per cent of it in contributions tax, or $900 — far less than the $2400 she would pay in income tax. This immediate tax benefit on the contribution is then compounded by the further tax benefit of a lower tax on the earnings of the investments while in superannuation. The fund pays tax of 15 per cent (at most) on the earnings rather than being taxed at her marginal rate if the investment was held outside superannuation.

To start some pre-tax contributions, you should talk to your employer's payroll person and ask for help to set up a regular contribution out of your pre-tax pay.

The cut-off point for whether you are better off making pre-tax contributions or post-tax contributions to your superannuation fund is dependent on your particular circumstances, but as a general rule if your salary is more than the co-contribution cut-off level then you should be looking at pre-tax contributions.

## Strategy 4: delay retirement

The idea of delaying retirement is a horrible one for many people, but in this case we are not necessarily talking about continuing to work full time beyond your planned retirement date, but rather about a transition to retirement that may be done over several years. There are two main benefits that can apply by doing this.

## Increase the years of investment

People in the 40 to 55 age bracket represent the tail end of the baby boomer generation and the front edge of generation X. As the bulk of the baby boomers retire and move out of the workforce there will almost certainly be a skills and experience gap developing. There is strong evidence that employers will want to encourage people with experience to work longer to help fill this gap.

In many cases, people who are between 40 and 55 now will have the ability to seek continuing employment beyond 65 on favourable terms, such as part time or with additional holiday periods.

One of the advantages that people will get by doing this is that it will delay the start of the period where they will be living off their superannuation — the pension draw down phase. This in turn means that the superannuation continues to grow with both contributions and investment earnings.

## Reduce the years of pension draw downs

The delay of pension draw downs has an additional benefit in that the period of draw downs that we will need will also reduce. Delaying our full retirement of course does not mean that we also get an extension in how long we will live. A female currently aged 65 has a life expectancy of 21.2 years. If she was 70 her life expectancy would be a further 17.1 years.

By transitioning to retirement over five years from 65 to 70 you get a double whammy effect on your superannuation. In Felicity's case it will increase the investment and contribution period by five years and reduce the pension draw down period by four years.

Let's go back to Felicity's situation and see what impact this will have. We move ahead 15 years to Felicity's 65th birthday. She has accumulated $546 000 (in today's dollars) in superannuation. She decides to transition to full-time retirement over the next five years, from age 65 to 70, and continues to work part time while earning 80 per cent of her pay at that point. Her annual pre-tax salary drops to $80 000 and post-tax pay is $62 000.

She is now bringing home less than she was while on full-time pay so she stops making additional pre-tax contributions to her superannuation account. We will also change her investment type to a balanced option. Given that she is relatively close to retirement, this option is more appropriate and will have less volatility in the lead up to commencing her draw down phase. You could argue that a large part of her superannuation assets will not be used in the short to medium term, but we are allowing for a reduction in her risk tolerance here, given the proximity of the start of her full reliance on her superannuation.

By the time she reaches 70, her superannuation account will be approximately $678 000. This would provide her with a pension income for the next 18 years of $52 500 per annum. We have now managed to get Felicity's post-retirement income up to 71 per cent of her full-time, pre–transition to retirement income and 84 per cent of her final pre-retirement income.

While not quite where it needs to be in order to maintain lifestyle, this result is double what Felicity could have expected before she started to use the strategies outlined above and therefore a very significant improvement on her prospects. In chapter 5 we will look at an additional pre-retirement strategy that may be able to help even further.

## Strategy 5: get advice

No matter how good the websites, calculators, written communication material and education seminars, personalised advice should be better. If the advice is coming from a qualified expert, with your best interests at heart, there is no better way to get your own situation and needs fully explained and solutions explored. You can access financial advice through most superannuation funds these days, including industry funds.

If you are in a retail fund or part of a small employer group within an employer superannuation master trust then there is a good chance that you may be charged an adviser service fee each year. This will be shown on your annual statement if it is the case, along with contact details for your adviser. If you are being charged such a fee, it may be worthwhile talking to the adviser about your own situation and what sort of help he or she can provide you with for the service fee and how much extra it would cost to get more comprehensive advice.

Do your research though and ensure that if you do decide to get additional advice it is from someone appropriately qualified, and that the advice won't be conflicted via commissions received for recommending certain products. We explore the best ways to get advice in chapter 7.

## Strategy 6: bank your winnings

Felicity's situation was clearly one of needing improvement. The circumstances that led her to that situation haven't been explored but they are generally going to be a combination of things that come down to a lack of involvement and understanding of her superannuation, which in turn led to poor or no investment choices, and periods of low or no contributions.

Equally there will be people who have managed their superannuation well through the early stages of their careers and get to this middle stage with the prospect of being ahead of the game in terms of tracking towards a comfortable retirement. If you have managed your superannuation accounts well through your early working life, you may now be tracking towards a post-retirement income in excess of your estimated pre-retirement income.

As we have seen, real life doesn't follow the nice smooth path of projection tools. Investments will go up faster during times of growth and fall back during bear markets, as we had in 2008. As part of doing a regular review of your superannuation account, it is worthwhile to run a projection of where you might wind up when you plan to retire. It would be a good practice to do this each time you receive your annual statement from your superannuation fund.

If you had done this after receiving your 2007 statement you could well have been in a situation where you were tracking well ahead of plan. When you do see that you are ahead of plan, it will allow you to exercise some options.

If the good news from the investment markets continues indefinitely then this may mean that you will be able to retire earlier. Or you could cut back on your additional contributions or you could look forward to a higher income in retirement than you currently plan to enjoy.

But all of these options are based on the idea that your long-term investment performance will stay ahead of the long-term average. A more realistic view is that a favourable position at the end of 2007 is as a result of an investment bubble — a period where the markets have got ahead of the long-term average, and the more likely future is one of a market correction.

Rather than ride the bubble without reference to the increasing probability of a correction, you could decide to 'bank your winnings'.

## De-risk

If your long-term target is to have a post-retirement income of 80 per cent of your pre-retirement income and your projections indicate that you are ahead of that plan, you can look at de-risking the superannuation account. For example, if you have $350 000 in your account but your retirement plans mean that you only need about $250 000 at that point, then the additional money means that you have the ability to achieve your long-term goals with a lower level of risk.

You can use the FIDO superannuation and pension calculator to see how you are going compared to your plan. First use the calculators as we did in the case study for Felicity. Rather than Felicity's numbers, plug in your own to see what sort of pension benefit you are tracking towards. If the pension income is between 70 per cent and 90 per cent of your current pre-tax salary then you are on track. If it is above 90 per cent then you are ahead and can look at de-risking.

Remember that our fundamental position for an investment strategy is to understand our goals, our time frames and our risk tolerance. Within the development of the strategy there is a premise that for any two choices of investment that deliver the same outcome, we should always go with the option that has the lowest risk.

In our example, the additional money may indicate that the retirement plans can be achieved with a long-term return of 6 per cent per annum before fees and taxes, rather than the 9 per cent that we are expecting out of a high-growth option. This means that you could use a moderately conservative investment option rather than the riskier high-growth option and still achieve your retirement goals.

By changing to a moderately conservative option, you halve the amount of growth assets in your superannuation investment portfolio. This in turn means that you halve the impact of any market correction when it happens.

In the wake of 2008, it would seem unlikely that many people are ahead of plan, however many people would have been ahead of plan in the middle of 2007. Clearly we can't go backwards in time to 2007, but the point is that there will be new periods of high returns in the future and these will be followed by corrections. As part of doing a regular review of your superannuation and other investments, there will be times when you realise that you are ahead of where you need to be. If you can muster the fortitude to recognise these times, and not get greedy with the options that they may mistakenly convince you will exist if the market doesn't correct, then you can de-risk your investments and still get to your goals.

When the market corrections do occur — depending on the level of correction — you may well then need to change your investment option again, if the investment return you require to achieve your goals can no longer be provided by the 'safer' investment option. But by banking your winnings as you go, you won't have to increase your return requirements—and therefore risk levels—to the same degree that you would have if you had simply let the money run.

## Strategy 7: get more out of your superannuation

The strategies that we have looked at so far are all about how to better grow your superannuation account. There are a few other things that you can do to get more out of your superannuation.

### Insurance

Life insurance is another element of superannuation funds that can really make a difference to how much value you get from your fund. As a general rule, most working Australians should take out their life insurance through their superannuation fund. In fact, it is fair to say that if you have a personal life insurance policy as well as a separate superannuation fund, you may very well be throwing money away.

Life insurance premiums are tax deductible to the superannuation fund, and most will either pass the tax deduction on to members or take it into account when setting premiums for their members. The premiums for personal life insurance policies are generally not tax deductible to a PAYG taxpayer. If your marginal income tax rate is higher than 15 per cent (if you earn more than $34 000 per annum for the 2008/09 tax year), you could get an immediate tax benefit by having your life insurance in your superannuation fund.

Superannuation funds can generally buy insurance in a wholesale market and at group rates. The underlying cost of the insurance can therefore be cheaper than if you approached an insurance company directly. In addition, the premiums effectively come out of your superannuation contributions, so the cost of the premiums doesn't have to be covered by your net pay. That doesn't mean that it's free — obviously the insurance premiums paid out reduce the end superannuation benefit, but if you have life insurance then the net cost to you will almost certainly be less if you run it through your superannuation fund.

The combination of all of these elements means that those on the top marginal tax rate may be able to save between 40 per cent and 60 per cent of the net cost of their life insurance premiums if they move their insurance into their superannuation fund.

Remember that when comparing fees and services between superannuation funds you also need to compare the cost of life insurance between superannuation funds. Quite often the differences in premiums charged for life insurance can vary more than the difference in administration fees.

If you have a big mortgage and dependants then you probably need between seven and 10 times your annual pay to be properly covered. The cost of this level of cover can be in the thousands of dollars a year, so these savings can be significant. It is therefore worth spending some time here on how much insurance you should have.

There are a lot of websites offering help on how much life insurance you should have. You do need to exert some care with these sites as they are often provided by either insurance companies or by insurance broking or advice businesses, and therefore there may be some benefits to these organisations in encouraging high levels of cover. That said, Australians are generally considered to be underinsured in terms of life insurance.

Your superannuation fund may have come with a default level of insurance cover. This is a level of cover that you receive automatically when you join the fund. While this is a helpful start, these default levels of cover are generally less than the true insurance needs that you may have. Your superannuation fund may offer a self-help calculator to assist with this.

The better websites will generally ask you to put in more details, as the more details you put in the more the answer is tailored to your situation. The good ones also help you understand what it is you are trying to cover. One of these better ones is on the BT Financial Group website <www.bt.com.au/investors/>.

The starting position for working it out yourself is to try to determine the impact on your family or partner if you were to die. This needs to take into account not only the loss of your existing and future income, but also any existing mortgages or debts that become difficult to pay if you were to die. It is not just about employed partners either. If one of you is not employed, but is bringing up children for example, you should also consider the cost of child care and home maintenance if that partner were to die.

If you don't have dependants or a partner, your life insurance needs may be considerably less.

## Strategy 8: plan to deal with periods of no contributions

For most working Australians there will be a time where you or your current or future partner will experience either a period outside the paid workforce or a period where there is only one income coming into the household. The cause — whether it is for raising children, being between jobs, being single or divorced, or something worse like ill health or injury — is largely irrelevant in terms of understanding and dealing with the implications for your retirement. The critical thing is to acknowledge that there is a high probability that a period without two incomes will occur and to do some planning that allows for this situation.

The best strategy for dealing with this is to expect that this will happen at some point and to acknowledge that during these periods superannuation contributions will most likely stop for the person not working. Getting our superannuation ahead of the game during the periods of plenty is a logical and viable approach to dealing with this. If damage has already happened, the alternative is that you need to find a way to catch up.

You would be surprised as to how much of a difference being out of the workforce for even a relatively short time can make. We saw in chapter 3 that a five-year reduction in a full 40-year working career can reduce the total amount accumulated in superannuation by over 20 per cent.

If you or your partner are experiencing periods without pay then you should try to make allowance for this by using other strategies to help make up for these periods. Additional contributions to the partner having a break from paid work can commence once that person ceases paid work, thereby allowing you to maximise the government co-contribution benefit.

Clearly there may be some periods without pay that can't be planned — especially as a result of illness or injury, or redundancy. The economic downturn that followed 2008 brought this home to many people around the world, and while this caused hardship for many people there is a fundamental lesson here around planning for the future. It is effectively a poor plan that relies on the assumption that the best outcome will always happen. In so many other parts of our lives, we realistically assess the upsides and downsides of a particular course of action. This can be within something as simple as driving through a red light because we are late, to insuring our house against the threat of fire.

And yet we rarely apply the same logic to long-range impacts of something that might be a virtual certainty, like reductions in family income due to periods where one partner may be out of paid work.

## Summary of strategies

Table 4.3 summarises the financial value of all of the strategies we have looked at for Felicity who earns $100 000 per annum pre tax.

## Plan B

As with every good set of strategies, you should also consider whether there is an alternative way of achieving your goals. Let's try to find some other ways that you might be able to secure a comfortable retirement lifestyle, and then you can evaluate the probability of success and the potential pitfalls of adopting these strategies (see table 4.4 on page 85).

As you can see, even if you are only now realising that your superannuation needs some serious help, there is still plenty that you can do to get your superannuation back on track. In our case study we have seen strategies that have doubled the value of a superannuation account.

**Table 4.3: strategy summary from 40 to 55**

| | Strategy | Estimated lump sum | Estimated income or pension | Proportion of pre-retirement salary after tax ($74 000 pa) |
|---|---|---|---|---|
| 1 | Consolidate superannuation accounts | Dependent on the number of accounts and fees charged; $47 000 better off in the example used. | | |
| 2a | Do nothing — balanced investment option | $394 000 | $26 700 pa from age 65 | 36% |
| 2b | Change investments to cash as a result of the 2008 sharemarket collapse | $300 000 at age 65 | $15 800 pa from age 65 | 21% |
| 2c | Change investments to high growth despite the 2008 sharemarket collapse | $439 000 at age 65 | $29 900 pa from age 65 | 40% |
| 2c & 3 | Make additional pre-tax contributions of 6 per cent of salary | $546 000 at age 65 | $37 000 pa from age 65 | 50% |

**Table 4.3 *(cont'd)*: strategy summary from 40 to 55**

| Strategy | | Estimated lump sum | Estimated income or pension | Proportion of pre-retirement salary after tax ($74 000 pa) |
|---|---|---|---|---|
| 2c, 3 & 4 | Delay retirement | $678 000 at age 70 | $62 000 pa from age 65<br>$52 500 pa from age 70 | 84%<br>71% |
| 5 | Get advice | This is your period of peak earning capacity and you can still use all of the strategies to your advantage. Getting advice can help you optimise your superannuation and ensure that you are getting all you can from it. | | |
| 6 | Bank your winnings | If you get ahead, don't assume that the markets will always be kind to you. | | |
| 7 | Get more out of your super | Make sure that you understand all of the potential benefits and services available through your fund. Look at the insurance rates and look at whether you need to plan for periods where there will be no contributions being paid. | | |

**Table 4.4: plan B strategies from 40 to 55**

| Plan B strategy | Description | Risks and potential outcomes |
|---|---|---|
| Invest outside of superannuation | Invest in a residential investment property | This is a very common form of investment, and the traditional benefits compared to superannuation have been the tax benefits if the investment is negatively geared, no requirement to preserve the investment until retirement, and the perceived 'realness' of bricks and mortar. Despite this, let's not forget that preservation is a moot point as we are looking at alternatives to super for the express purpose of funding for retirement, and bricks and mortar are just as 'real' inside a superannuation fund as outside. At a headline level if preservation is not an issue and you can have the same or similar investments inside or outside a superannuation fund, the vehicle that offers the lowest tariff (taxes and fees) should provide you with the best outcome. |
| Start a business and sell it for a motza | You create a business phenomenon and sell it for millions | The small to medium enterprise business is actually a very significant and important part of our country's social and economic structure. That said, the majority of these businesses simply provide a reasonable income to the proprietors and have limited ability to be sold for more than the wholesale value of real assets, once those proprietors are no longer involved in the business. |
| Rely on inheritance | Wait until your parents die and live off the remainder of their estate | At least one of your parents lives well into their 80s or 90s and has to sell the house in order to live out their remaining years, leaving you too little, too late. |

It is a relatively simple thing for you to harness these strategies, and if you do so you will be able to easily and dramatically enhance your retirement lifestyle.

The longer you leave it though, the harder it gets to fix. For a clue on just how hard it can get it is worth having a read of the next chapters. As well as making it clearer as to just how lucky you are as a result of starting early, you will see that there are some strategies worth looking at for people in older age brackets that have managed to get ahead of the game, and how to lock in some of those benefits.

## The next step

The action plan for you is relatively simple and it can be done in steps:

1 Consolidate — get your superannuation all in one good fund that suits you.
2 Choose your investment strategy — time is still on your side and this allows you to look at risk differently.
3 Make additional regular contributions to your fund — this may be the period of your peak earning power and some of it needs to be put aside for the future.
4 Do a regular review of how your fund is tracking to your retirement goals — bank your winnings when you get ahead.
5 Use your fund's services — look at your life insurance needs, review the education services and think about getting financial advice.
6 Read the next chapter to see how pre-retirement planning can make a difference.

# Chapter 5

## Where to from here — from 55 to retirement

Retirement can be something we approach with anticipation or dread. In some cases it will be our financial preparedness or the strength of our desire to keep working or not that may drive these emotions.

For most people, the lead up to retirement is still a period where financial security can be cemented, or it can be a period where hard questions need to be asked and answered. Time in terms of its ability to help build wealth is now losing its power, but it can still help dramatically in terms of maintaining wealth. If there are gaps in our financial security then perhaps not insignificant sacrifices may be required.

On the plus side, this can often be a period where our lifestyle costs are reducing. A combination of a hopefully paid off mortgage and children out of home should mean lower living costs. The challenge stems from whether those reductions in living costs have been converted to investing in the future or simply redirected into other lifestyle opportunities such as travel, home upgrades or cars.

Clearly people in this group should have some superannuation already accumulated, and there is a very good chance that they will have seen their superannuation badly affected by the events of 2008. Once you have seen your superannuation account balance hit by something like the Global Financial Crisis, there is often a temptation to shift the remaining balance to a more conservative, 'safe' investment option such as cash. As you will see from the strategies outlined below, this could be one of the worst things you could do.

In the earlier chapters you will have seen that to secure financial independence in retirement you need to understand your starting position and your end goals and time frames. You will have developed a sense of whether you are prepared to take on volatility of returns in order to achieve those goals with more certainty and speed, or whether you will be more comfortable taking longer to get there for a smoother ride. You will have an understanding of how much money you will need to make your retirement financially secure.

In this age bracket you have three weapons to secure financial security. Time — while diminished compared to the people in younger age groups — can still be used to your advantage. The other main weapons will be to acknowledge and use your continuing peak earning capacity wisely and to maximise the value extracted from reducing living costs caused by mortgages being paid off and children becoming independent.

There is potentially a real challenge for people in this age group who have only had the benefit of superannuation contributions since the introduction of the superannuation guarantee system in 1992. For 60 year olds that might mean that their current superannuation balance is the result of less than 20 years of contributions — half of that going to be experienced by most people currently under age 40. That gap cannot be realistically solved solely by reducing lifestyle costs to a point where catch up contributions are sufficient.

Despite these potential problems, there are some strategies that you can use to generate some significant improvements to the situation.

## Understand the journey

Before we launch into strategies, you should revisit the journey you are trying to make. This means making sure that you know where you are now, where you are trying to get to and how long you can take to get there. As with any journey, it is often important to make the most of the travel rather than making the destination the single important element.

Any process of saving or investing for the future must by definition have an element of present-day sacrifice. If you haven't done this early in your working life, the amount you will have to save out of current income will be larger.

We should keep in mind that the end result is about lifestyle, not a specific dollar amount. We use dollars as a means of quantifying the cost of the desired lifestyle, and we do this by converting the superannuation account balance at retirement into a post-retirement income. The methodology for the conversion is complicated and takes into account many assumptions about how long you are expected to live, the investment returns on your superannuation balance while in retirement, and cost of living increases.

As a way of trying to get a handle on lifestyle results, we try to understand the difference between pre-retirement salary and post-retirement salary. If your lifestyle immediately prior to retirement costs $80 000 a year in today's after-tax dollars, maintenance of that lifestyle after retirement is going to cost a similar amount. There are some aspects of retired life that are less costly compared to pre-retirement, such as travel to work, clothing and fast food. In addition, there are tax breaks on income you receive once you are retired which mean that you don't have to earn as much to maintain the same level of after-tax income. That said, there may be other expense lines that increase in retirement, such as travel, hobbies and health care.

We can therefore reflect the success (or otherwise) of these strategies by showing the post-retirement salary as a percentage of your pre-retirement salary. Any strategy that delivers a post-retirement salary result of better than 70 per cent of pre-retirement salary is generally going to be worth a look.

## Strategy 1: consolidation and fee management

Just like other forms of investments and financial products, superannuation accounts have fees. If you have lots of accounts you wind up being charged lots of fees. The total amount of fees you may be paying will depend on the number of accounts you have and the types of fees those funds charge.

As a result of the superannuation guarantee legislation that came into effect in 1992, every employer you have had since then has had to make superannuation contributions to a fund. Up until recently, the employer could control which fund was used, and therefore it was easy to collect lots of superannuation accounts as you moved from employer to employer.

In 2005, the rules were changed to allow you to tell your employer to make your superannuation contributions to a fund of your choice. This meant that you could then choose a fund that would suit you over the long term, and ask each of your employers to make all contributions to that fund.

We need to recognise that if you have reached this point of your working life you may have had a large number of jobs and employers and, therefore, superannuation accounts. If you didn't go to the trouble of consolidating those accounts as you left each employer then the damage caused by paying multiple sets of account-keeping fees may already have been done.

You won't be alone with this problem. Since compulsory superannuation was introduced in 1992, it is estimated that there are at least 13 million unnecessary superannuation accounts. Even worse is the number of lost accounts — over six million. Lost superannuation accounts are accounts where the superannuation fund has completely lost contact with the owner of the account. These lost accounts have nearly $13 billion in them as at 2008. That is one lost account for every two working Australians.

If you are not sure that you know where all of your superannuation is, go back to chapter 2 and read the section on 'Where is your superannuation?' for some helpful hints on how to track it all down.

While the fee damage may already be done, it is still worthwhile consolidating your superannuation accounts. It will stop further unnecessary costs being charged on your superannuation and, more importantly, it will make your super much easier to manage if it is all in one primary account.

Another important thing to remember when comparing superannuation funds is the cost of insurance. This can vary a lot between funds, to the point that the insurance differences can outweigh the administration fee differences, especially if you have a large amount of life insurance cover and are in your more mature years. For example, according to research by Chant West that looks at 33 major superannuation funds, the median annual cost of death and total and permanent disability insurance for a 59-year-old male working in a white-collar job is $12.11 per $1000 of cover. If that person wanted $500 000 of cover, the median cost would be $6055 a year. The cheapest cover available out of that group of funds (same cover level) is only $1970, while the dearest was a whopping $13 500. The difference in premium between the cheapest and dearest fund for this level of insurance cover is over $11 000 a year.

It is therefore important to have in mind the amount of life insurance cover you need — as opposed to the amount of cover you currently have — when you are making your fund comparisons.

Transferring your superannuation account balance from one fund to another is relatively easy (though harder than transferring money from one bank to another), but there may be real issues in transferring your life insurance from one fund to another — especially as you get older.

In many cases, you will need to reapply for your life insurance cover in the new fund. This may mean that you will have to complete medical questionnaires and may even need to have a medical examination with a doctor. If your health has deteriorated since getting cover in your old fund, you may not be able to get the same or an appropriate level of cover in the new fund. It is therefore very important to get your insurance cover set up in your new fund before you cancel your cover in the old fund.

If it turns out to be too difficult to transfer your insurance arrangements, or if one of your old funds has very good insurance that can't be matched in your new preferred superannuation fund, consider leaving those insurance arrangements in place with a nominal amount of your superannuation in the fund to cover the cost of the insurance premiums. You will need to take this extra superannuation fund into account when dealing with other aspects of your superannuation strategy, however the inconvenience of two funds compared to one may be worthwhile for the sake of the better insurance arrangements.

## Strategy 2: Choose your investment option

Now that you are in this critical final stage of your superannuation accumulation, you really need to ensure that you are wringing every last bit out of your superannuation fund. Getting the best performance out of your fund is an essential part of this optimisation process.

It isn't just about fees. The consolidation strategy highlights that for two funds that deliver the same performance the one with the lowest fees will produce a better result. Fee differences between superannuation funds can be as high as 1.5 per cent per annum of the assets. But picking the right investment option can make double this difference.

Most funds will segment their investment options into one of six or so categories based on a risk versus return profile:

- *Cash:* 100 per cent invested in cash or similar securities.
- *Conservative:* Approximately 30 per cent invested in growth-style investments (Australian shares, international shares and property) and 70 per cent invested in income-style investments (cash, Australian fixed interest or bonds and international fixed interest).
- *Moderately conservative:* Approximately 50 per cent invested in growth-style investments and 50 per cent invested in income-style investments.
- *Balanced:* Approximately 70 per cent invested in growth-style investments and 30 per cent invested in income-style investments.
- *Growth:* Approximately 85 per cent invested in growth-style investments and 15 per cent invested in income-style investments.
- *High growth:* Approximately 95 per cent invested in growth-style investments. Some small amounts of cash may exist as a result of cash flow requirements.

Funds differ in how they describe their options. Some funds will call 50 per cent growth/50 per cent income a balanced option, while other funds will call 70 per cent growth/ 30 per cent income a balanced option. The important thing is the amount of growth assets (shares or property) versus the amount of income or defensive assets (fixed interest and cash), rather than the name of the investment option. I have used the asset allocations shown above for all projections in this book.

The cash option will offer a low long-term return with low volatility (or risk). In contrast, the high-growth option will generally achieve the highest long-term return, however it will have higher volatility over shorter periods. The other options fall in between in terms of both return and volatility.

There is an important thing to note here and that is the word 'generally'. You can show data that reveals over a specific 10-year period some of the more conservative options outperform the high-growth options — the 10 years between 1 January 1999 and 31 December 2008 for example.

*Generally* the more growth assets your investments contain, the higher return you will receive over the long term. For projections we need to use an estimate of investment performance in the future. The projections used in our case studies use estimated future investment performance supplied by ASIC (as shown in table 5.1).

**Table 5.1: estimated future investment performance**

| Investment option | Estimate of future long-term (10+ years) investment performance before tax and fees |
|---|---|
| High-growth option (95% growth assets) | 9.0% pa |
| Growth option (85% growth assets) | 8.5% pa |
| Balanced option (70% growth assets) | 8.0% pa |
| Conservative option (35% growth assets) | 6.0% pa |
| Capital stable or cash (0% growth assets) | 5.5% pa |

*Source:* FIDO and Chant West.

In addition, most funds offer you not only a choice of investments around a risk and return profile, but also different fund managers and even individual company securities.

Don't forget that even though you may be within 10 years of your planned retirement date, the bulk of your superannuation balance will have to last you much longer than this — probably for at least 20 years beyond age 65. So time is still a factor, and you need to have a long-term view for the majority of your superannuation assets.

## Balanced option

John is 60 and has an existing superannuation balance of $150 000, and his salary is $80 000 a year pre-tax or $62 000 a year post-tax. He has made no active investment choice with his superannuation fund so his employer contributions are being invested in the default investment option, which is a balanced option. He is making no additional contributions, so the employer superannuation guarantee contributions — 9 per cent of his pay — are the only contributions being made.

Using the FIDO superannuation calculator you can see that John will have an estimated superannuation account balance of $210 000 (in today's dollars) by the time he gets to age 65.

The FIDO pension calculator shows that if John invests this $210 000 into a term allocated pension for the same term as his life expectancy, he will receive a pension income of about $16 200 a year — or 26 per cent of his pre-retirement income after tax. Not a great result, and one that would almost certainly cause a very significant reduction in John's lifestyle.

A term allocated pension is a retirement product that will pay out a reasonably stable income over a target time period.

We can use the term allocated pension calculator to estimate how long a normal allocated pension will last given a particular starting balance and income draw down levels. Alternatively you can use it to estimate how much income you can get out of an allocated pension given a particular starting balance and term.

A male aged 65 at 2008 has a life expectancy of 17.7 years, so using a term of 18 years in a term allocated pension calculator is a good guide to working out how much income a male will have in retirement if he retires at 65. A female's life expectancy at the same point is 21.2 years and post-retirement income would be about $14 200 a year.

The $80 000 salary is clearly just an example. The FIDO calculator uses one salary level and indexes that salary for inflation only. The reality of course is that people will have different pay outcomes throughout their working life. The important thing here is not how close or far the $80 000 is from reality, but rather the extent of difference between the post-retirement salary and the pre-retirement salary.

While you may think that the example here is extreme, the statistics on the size of average member superannuation accounts are scarily low. Table 5.2 (overleaf) shows the average member superannuation balance at 30 June 2008. These numbers are the consolidated member balances — not average account balances which are even lower as they reflect the fact that many people have more than one superannuation account.

The average member superannuation account balances are a consequence of both the number of years of contributions and the salary of the members. In John's case we have recognised that his current salary of $80 000 is higher than the average salary in Australia and therefore we have assumed that his superannuation account balance would be higher than the average member balance for a male of his age.

**Table 5.2: average member balances at 30 June 2008**

| Age group | Males | Females |
|---|---|---|
| 50 to 55 | $135 900 | $75 500 |

*Source:* Rice Warner Research.

Women generally have lower account balances than men of similar age. The combination of superannuation contributions not being made available for many women until the commencement of the superannuation guarantee in 1992, a higher proportion of women doing part-time work and broken periods of paid employment to bring up children mean that many women on average have lower account balances. Unfortunately the problem is compounded because women have a longer life expectancy than men. This means that they need a larger superannuation account balance to maintain lifestyle, because women on average will live longer than men and therefore be retired for longer.

## Cash option

If John switches his superannuation into the cash option as a result of the 2008 sharemarket collapse rather than leave it in the balanced option over the remaining five years of his working life, his superannuation benefit would most likely be around $189 000.

## High-growth option

On the other hand, if John switches to a high-growth investment option for the remaining five years of his working life then his superannuation benefit would most likely be around $218 000.

Due to the relatively small amount of time left to retirement, on the face of it the investment choice does not appear to make a big difference — only around $30 000. But relative to the total balance this is over 15 per cent, and in John's case every bit helps.

More to the point though is that not all of John's superannuation account balance will be used when he retires. In fact, most of it will be spread out over the rest of his life, which still allows for time and compound interest to work some magic.

The thing to note here is that while switching to a high-growth option is helping, it is not going to fix the main problem that John faces and that is a significant shortfall in retirement funding. In this situation he is going to have to apply a series of strategies to try to fix the problem — there is no single silver bullet. Getting the most out of the investment performance is going to be one of those important steps, and while you might be concerned that there is higher risk with this approach, you should remember that having time up your sleeve changes the way we look at risk.

## Strategy 3: make regular additional contributions

John has decided that while changing his investment strategy to a high-growth option will be worth doing, he clearly needs to do more in order to have a better retirement outcome than 26 per cent of his pre-retirement pay. He decides to make a regular monthly additional contribution of 10 per cent of his pre-tax salary (or $8000 in the first year) for the remaining five years before retiring. This equates to about $670 per month of his pre-tax income in the first year, but it will go up in line with any salary increases in the future.

It is worth noting that as 10 per cent is coming out of his pre-tax pay, it will be only a 9 per cent reduction in his total after-tax pay. This is because the $8000 that he is contributing to superannuation would normally be taxed at his marginal tax rate of 30 per cent rather than his average tax rate of 23 per cent.

The FIDO superannuation calculator estimates that his superannuation account balance will now be around $256 000 at age 65, with an average post-retirement salary of $19 800 or 32 per cent of pre-retirement salary. Again that is in today's dollars after tax.

This represents an additional $70 000 on top of what John would have achieved if he had switched his superannuation to cash following the 2008 sharemarket collapse. Putting 10 per cent of his after-tax pay into superannuation may be difficult, but we need to face up to the challenge that doing nothing will result in a very poor retirement outcome for John. The combination of strategies 2 and 3 has so far gained John nearly 40 per cent extra in his superannuation account, but his retirement lifestyle is going to be based on a post-retirement income of only 32 per cent of his pre-retirement income — he needs to find more.

## Co-contributions

If you earn less than $60 342 in the 2008/09 year, and you make an after-tax contribution, the government will also make a contribution to your superannuation account. If you earn less than $30 342 in the 2008/09 year, the government will contribute $1.50 for every extra dollar that you put in up to a maximum co-contribution of $1500 a year. The amount of money that the government contributes for you reduces as you earn more money above the $30 342 threshold, and cuts out completely once you earn more than $60 342 per annum. These salary thresholds are indexed each year at 30 June.

This strategy is one of those absolute 'no brainers' that you get to hear about every now and then. In effect, the government will give you money simply because you save a little bit for your own future — what a great scheme!

As a result of the 2009 Federal Budget, this maximum co-contribution rate will temporarily reduce for the five years between 1 July 2009 to 30 June 2014, but this temporary reduction doesn't make a significant difference to the end result and it is still a great benefit.

You don't have to apply for these government contributions either. If you make after-tax contributions to your superannuation fund, the fund will report those contributions to the Tax Office and the government will then make the co-contribution directly into your superannuation fund for you.

The only crazy thing here is the number of Australians that don't use it.

As John's salary is over the co-contribution salary threshold, he doesn't benefit from this scheme, but being on a higher tax bracket means that he can generate real tax savings by making his contributions pre-tax.

## Pre-tax or post-tax contributions

If you earn more than the co-contribution cut-off salary ($60 342 per annum in the 2008/09 year), the strategy of making extra contributions still holds. With a higher salary, though, you may be better off making your additional regular contributions through a pre-tax arrangement or salary sacrifice. This simply means that you direct some of your pre-tax income into your superannuation fund. This income then gets taxed at the superannuation tax rate, which is lower than your marginal tax rate.

In John's case his annual salary is $80 000 so his marginal rate is 30 per cent—every dollar that he earns over $34 000 is taxed by 30¢. The tax he pays on the last $8000 he earns in the year is $2400 (ignoring the Medicare levy). By diverting that $8000 into superannuation he loses only 15 per cent of it in contributions tax, or $1200—half the $2400 he would pay in income tax. This immediate tax benefit on the contribution is then compounded by the further tax benefit of a lower tax on the earnings of the investments while in superannuation. The fund pays tax of 15 per cent (at most) on the earnings rather than being taxed at his marginal rate if the investment was held outside of superannuation.

To start some pre-tax contributions, you should talk to your employer's payroll person and ask for help to set up a regular contribution out of your pre-tax pay.

The cut-off point for whether you are better off making pre-tax contributions or post-tax contributions to your super fund is dependent on your particular circumstances, but as a general rule if your salary is more than the co-contribution cut-off level then you should be looking at pre-tax contributions.

## Strategy 4: delay retirement

The idea of delaying retirement is a horrible one for many people, but in this case we are not necessarily talking about continuing to work full time beyond your planned retirement date, but rather about a transition to retirement that may be done over several years. There are two main benefits that can apply by doing this.

## Increase the years of investment

People in the 55 to 65 age bracket are part of the baby boomer generation. As the bulk of the baby boomers retire and move out of the workforce there will almost certainly be skills and experience gaps developing. There is strong evidence that employers will want to encourage people with experience to work longer to help fill this gap.

In many cases people in this situation will have the ability to seek continuing employment beyond 65 on favourable terms, such as part time or with additional holiday periods.

One of the advantages that people will get by doing this is that it will delay the start of the period where they will be living off their superannuation — the pension draw down phase. This in turn means that the superannuation continues to grow with both contributions and investment earnings.

## Reduce the years of pension draw downs

The delay of pension draw downs has an additional benefit in that the period of draw downs that we will need will also reduce. Delaying our full retirement of course does not mean that we also get an extension in how long we will live. A male currently aged 65 has a life expectancy of 17.7 years. If he was 70 his life expectancy would be a further 14.1 years.

By transitioning to retirement over five years from 65 to 70 you get a double whammy effect on your superannuation. In

John's case it will increase the investment and contribution period by five years and reduce the pension draw down period by three years.

Let's go back to John's situation and see what impact this will have. We move ahead five years to John's 65th birthday. He has accumulated $256 000 (in today's dollars) in superannuation. He decides to transition to full-time retirement over the next five years from age 65 to 70, and continues to work part time while earning 80 per cent of his pay at that point.

He is now bringing home less than he was while on full-time pay but he continues making additional contributions to his superannuation account at the rate of 10 per cent of his new reduced pay rate. Because his new pay rate is now less than the cut-off for the government co-contributions, he will make his additional contributions out of after-tax pay, rather than pre-tax.

We will also change his investment type to a balanced option. Given that he is relatively close to retirement this option is more appropriate and will have less volatility in the lead up to commencing his draw down phase. You could argue that a large part of his superannuation assets will not be used in the short to medium term, but we are allowing for a reduction in his risk tolerance here, given the proximity of the start of his full reliance on his superannuation.

By the time he reaches 70, his superannuation account will be approximately $363 000. This would provide him with a pension income for the next 15 years of $32 100 per annum. We have now managed to double John's expected superannuation balance at retirement using these three strategies. The result means that his post-retirement income is up from 26 per cent to 52 per cent of his full-time, pre–transition to retirement income and 63 per cent of his final pre-retirement income.

While not quite where it needs to be in order to maintain lifestyle, this result is double what John could have expected before he started to use the strategies outlined above and therefore a very significant improvement on his prospects.

## Strategy 5: transition to retirement tax strategy

A refinement to the above strategy comes about if you use a transition to retirement allocated pension. Since 2005, the government has allowed a transition to retirement strategy that has specific tax benefits. The strategy allows people between age 55 and 65 to start to access their existing superannuation balance in the form of an income stream while they continue to work. The primary purpose is to give people flexibility of income sources to allow the transition from full-time work to retirement over a longer period.

The tax benefit part of this strategy comes about if you can convert a larger portion of your salary into superannuation contributions, while living off the income coming out of your superannuation pension. In effect you convert your higher taxed salary into superannuation contributions that are taxed at a maximum rate of 15 per cent, and at the same time replace your salary income with pension income that is tax free. A specific product called a 'transition to retirement pension' is used for this.

If you are 65 or over, you don't need to use a special product — you can simply transfer your superannuation account balance to an allocated pension product and start drawing down an income from the allocated pension.

Meanwhile, you start a new superannuation account and direct as much money as you can out of your salary into the new superannuation fund.

As an example, we can look at John's situation at age 65 and consider how he might use this strategy as he transitions to retirement from age 65 to 70. You will recall that he had $256 000 in his superannuation account when he turned 65, and had decided to continue to work until age 70 but on a part-time basis that would mean his salary reduced to 80 per cent of his full-time rate — $64 000. He had also decided to continue to make after-tax contributions of 10 per cent of his after-tax pay, meaning that his take-home pay from his new salary after age 65 was $44 400. This strategy leads him to a superannuation account balance at age 70 of around $363 000 and an annual income after age 70 of around $32 100 after tax.

The alternative strategy requires him to convert his superannuation at age 65 to a pension based on his life expectancy of 18 years, which will pay him an annual tax-free salary of around $19 800. As his pension is paying him $19 800, he needs a further $24 600 to bring this up to $44 400 per annum after tax. He therefore decides to pay himself $27 900 per annum of his pre-tax salary (which gives him the required $24 600 after tax) and contributes the rest of his salary to a *new* superannuation account. The unused salary being contributed to the new superannuation account is equivalent to $36 100 per annum of pre-tax pay.

This strategy means that John can contribute a whopping $36 100 per annum of pre-tax salary to a new superannuation account, while still receiving a comfortable preretirement salary of $44 400 a year after tax. Given the salary levels, John should make the contributions using after-tax pay so that he can take advantage of the government co-contribution scheme. He therefore pays income tax on the $36 100 and contributes the resulting $25 600 after tax to his new superannuation account.

By the time he reaches 70, his new superannuation account will be worth around $166 000. This could pay him another pension for the rest of his life expectancy of 15 years of $14 600.

This second pension, when added to the first one, means that John will receive a combined pension of $34 400 per annum — higher than the $32 100 per annum that would have been achieved without the additional tax strategy benefit.

The combination of all of these strategies means that John now has an income stream of $34 400 per annum after tax, which is around 77 per cent of his transitional pre-retirement after-tax pay or 61 per cent of his full-time pre-retirement after-tax pay. In addition, John would almost certainly be eligible for a part Age Pension, which could further supplement his retirement income. We will look at how the Age Pension interacts with your superannuation pension in the next chapter.

This strategy works even better for people on higher incomes as this is where the greater tax benefits are generated. It is best to get financial advice if you are considering using this strategy.

## Strategy 6: get advice

No matter how good the websites, calculators, written communication material and education seminars, personalised advice should be better. If the advice is coming from a qualified expert, with your best interests at heart, then there is no better way to get your own situation and needs fully explained and solutions explored. You can access financial advice through most superannuation funds these days, including industry funds.

There is an 'if' in that last paragraph that does need to be explored, and ultimately there are degrees within the quality of advice you can receive. Clearly, an adviser needs to be appropriately licensed and have relevant qualifications. Another good rule of thumb is to determine who is paying the adviser — you or someone else.

If you are in a retail fund or part of a small employer group within an employer superannuation master trust then there is a good chance that you may be charged an adviser service fee each year. This will be shown on your annual statement if it is the case, along with contact details for your adviser. If you are being charged such a fee, it may be worthwhile talking to the adviser about your own situation and what sort of help he or she can provide you with for the service fee and how much extra it would cost to get more comprehensive advice.

Do your research though and ensure that if you do decide to get additional advice it is from someone appropriately qualified and that the advice won't be conflicted via commissions received for recommending certain products. At the end of the day you should feel happy to pay the adviser for his or her services rather than get a 'free' or heavily discounted service because the products that the adviser will place you in pay the adviser a commission. By making sure that you pay the adviser, you can have comfort that you will be told the best things for you to do, even if it doesn't involve an investment. One of the best examples of improving your financial security that doesn't involve an investment is to pay off your mortgage on your house, as the cost of this debt is generally not tax deductible.

This stage of your life, where you are still enjoying peak earning capacity and hopefully reduced costs, should mean that you have surplus income. The combination of surplus income and pending retirement means that good financial advice can make a real difference to how you will live in retirement.

The Financial Planning Association of Australia has a section on its website that can assist you to find a financial planner. It includes lists of planners by location as well as useful tips on questions to ask a planner in order to assess how well he or she will service you. Go to <www.fpa.asn.au/Findaplanner/>.

A full financial plan will generally cost from $2000, and in many cases it is money well spent.

## Strategy 7: bank your winnings

John's situation was clearly one of needing improvement. The circumstances that led him to that situation haven't been explored but they are generally going to be a combination of things that come down to a lack of involvement and understanding of his superannuation, which in turn led to poor or no investment choices, and periods of low or no contributions.

Equally there will be people who have managed their superannuation well through the earlier stages of their careers and get to this later stage with the prospect of being ahead of the game in terms of tracking towards a comfortable retirement.

As we have seen, real life doesn't follow the nice smooth path of projection tools. Investments will go up faster during times of growth and fall back during bear markets as we had in 2008. If you develop a practice of doing regular reviews of your super — say once a year when you receive your main annual fund statement — you will be able to see when you are ahead of your projected plan.

A good practice is to take the balance from your annual statement and then run your own projection on the FIDO superannuation and pension calculators. If the pension income is between 70 per cent and 90 per cent of your current pre-tax salary then you are on track. If it is above 90 per cent then you are ahead and can look at de-risking.

If the good news from the investment markets continues indefinitely then this may mean that you will be able to retire earlier. Or you could cut back on your additional contributions, or you could look forward to a higher income in retirement than you currently plan for.

But all of these options are based on the idea that your long-term investment performance will stay ahead of the long-term average. A more realistic view is that the favourable position is a result of an investment bubble — a period where the markets have got ahead of the long-term average, and the more likely future is one of a market correction. Clearly this is what happened in the years leading up to 2007.

Rather than ride the bubble without reference to the increasing probability of a correction, you could take the option of 'banking the winnings'.

Remember that our fundamental position for an investment strategy is to understand our goals, our time frames and our risk tolerance. Within the development of the strategy there is a premise that for any two choices of investment that deliver the same outcome, we should always go with the option that has the lowest risk.

By doing regular investment reviews of your superannuation, you can see situations where you have more money in your account than the long-term plan requires. This would then mean that you can achieve your goals with a lower level of risk. Your review may indicate that you can achieve your goals with, say, a 6 per cent long-term investment return compared to the 9 per cent return you may have thought you needed when making your original investment option decision. This means that you could use a moderately conservative investment option rather than the riskier high-growth option.

By changing to a moderately conservative option, you effectively halve the amount of growth assets in your superannuation portfolio. This in turn means that you reduce the impact of any market correction when it happens.

In the aftermath of 2008, there are very few people that are sitting in a position where their superannuation investments are ahead of plan. The point though is that there will be new periods of high return in the future and these will be followed by corrections. As part of doing a regular review of your superannuation and other investments, there will be times when you realise that you are ahead of where you need to be. If you can muster the fortitude to recognise these times and not get greedy with the options that they may mistakenly convince you will exist if the market doesn't correct, then you can de-risk your investments and still get to your goals.

When the market corrections do occur — depending on the level of correction — you may well then need to change your investment option again, if the investment return you require to achieve your goals can no longer be provided by the 'safer' investment option. But by banking your winnings as you go, you won't have to increase your return requirements — and therefore risk levels — to the same degree that you would have if you had simply let the money run.

## Strategy 8: get more out of your superannuation

The strategies that we have looked at so far are all about how to better grow your superannuation account. There are a few other things that you can do to get more out of your super.

### Insurance

We have looked at the reasons why you should consider using your superannuation fund for your life insurance in strategy 1: consolidation and fee management. The reasons are compelling. It is also worth spending some time here on how much insurance you should have.

There are a lot of websites offering help on how much life insurance you should have. You do need to exert some care with these sites as they are often provided by insurance companies or by insurance broking or advice businesses and therefore there may be some benefits to these organisations in encouraging high levels of cover. That said, Australians are generally considered to be underinsured in terms of life insurance.

Your superannuation fund may have come with a default level of insurance cover. This is a level of cover that you receive automatically when you join the fund. While this is a helpful start, these default levels of cover are generally less than the insurance level that you may need. Your superannuation fund may offer a self-help calculator to assist with this.

The better websites will generally ask you to put in more details, as the more details you put in the more the answer is tailored to your situation. The good ones also help you understand what it is you are trying to cover. One of these better ones is on the BT Financial Group website: <www.bt.com.au/investors/>.

The starting position for working it out yourself is to try to determine the impact on your family or partner if you were to die. This needs to take into account not only the loss of your existing and future income, but also any existing mortgages or debts that become difficult to pay if you were to die.

At this stage of your life, it is common to see life insurance needs reducing. If you have the house paid off and the children are now out of home and independent, your life insurance needs may revolve simply around the loss of income and continued savings ability to meet your partner's retirement goals.

If you don't have dependants or a partner, your life insurance needs may be considerably less.

## Summary of strategies

Table 5.3 (overleaf) summarises the financial value of all of the strategies we have looked at for John in the lead up to retirement — his income is $62 000 pre tax.

**Table 5.3: strategy summary from 55 to retirement**

| Strategy | | Estimated lump sum | Estimated income or pension | Proportion of pre-retirement salary after tax of $62 000 pa |
|---|---|---|---|---|
| 1 | Consolidate superannuation accounts | The damage of multiple accounts may already be done, but it is worth getting it all under control, in one primary account, and to check that you don't have any lost superannuation accounts. | | |
| 2a | Do nothing — use a balanced investment option | $210 000 at age 65 | $16 200 pa from age 65 | 26% |
| 2b | Change investments to cash as a result of the 2008 sharemarket collapse | $189 000 at age 65 | $11 900 pa from age 65 | 19% |
| 2c | Change investments to high growth despite the 2008 sharemarket collapse | $218 000 at age 65 | $16 800 pa from age 65 | 27% |

| Strategy | | Estimated lump sum | Estimated income or pension | Proportion of pre-retirement salary after tax of $62 000 pa |
|---|---|---|---|---|
| 2c & 3 | Make additional pre-tax contributions of 10 per cent of salary | $256 000 at age 65 | $19 800 pa from age 65 | 32% |
| 2c, 3 & 4 | Delay retirement | $363 000 at age 70 | $44 400 pa from age 65<br>$32 100 pa from age 70 | 72%<br>52% |
| 2c, 3, 4 & 5 | Transition to retirement | $256 000 at age 65 plus<br>$166 000 at age 70 | $44 400 pa from age 65<br>$34 400 pa from age 70 | 72%<br>55% |
| 6 | Get advice | The lead up to retirement is a critical period as this may help you cement all of the strategies as well as ensure you are looking at all of your retirement product options. | | |
| 7 | Bank your winnings | There will be periods of good investment returns in the future so a good practice will be to develop a habit of regular checking and risk reviews. | | |
| 8 | Get more out of your superannuation | Insurance may still be important and the cost differences between funds can be large. | | |

## Plan B

As with every good set of strategies, you should also consider whether there is an alternative way of achieving your goals. Let's try and find some other ways that you might be able to secure a comfortable retirement lifestyle, and then you can evaluate the probability of success and the potential pitfalls of adopting these strategies (see table 5.4 on page 117).

As you can see, even if you are only now realising that your superannuation needs some serious help, there is still plenty that you can do to help get your superannuation back on track. In our case study we have seen strategies that have doubled the value of superannuation.

## The next step

It is a relatively simple thing for you to harness these strategies, and if you do so you will be able to easily and dramatically enhance your retirement lifestyle:

1. Consolidate—get your superannuation all in one good fund that suits you.
2. Choose your investment strategy—time is still a factor as most of your superannuation assets will be used after your retirement.
3. Make additional regular contributions to your fund—you may be going through a period of reducing living costs with the mortgage paid off and children leaving home, and the surplus income may now be an essential element of getting your superannuation back on track.
4. Do a regular review of how your fund is tracking to your retirement goals—bank your winnings when you get ahead.

5 Use your fund's services — look at your life insurance needs, review the education services and think about getting financial advice.
6 Read the next chapter to see how even in retirement there are strategies that can help maintain lifestyle.

**Table 5.4: plan B strategies from 55 to retirement**

| Plan B strategy | Description | Risks and potential outcomes |
|---|---|---|
| Downsize the house | By selling the family home you can move to a smaller house or to a cheaper house in the country and live off the difference in property prices. | This will be a definite consideration for a lot of retirees. In effect it is all about releasing some of the built-up equity in your home. The trade-off will be around how much of the equity in your house can be freed up in the process and what sort of lifestyle impact will result. Another aspect of this strategy is to consider using a reverse mortgage. This is a bank product that allows the bank to pay you an income stream as they gradually take out a mortgage over your house. Your estate will be left with the mortgage on the house. |
| Win lotto | You 'invest' each week in a lottery, with the eventual proceeds securing your retirement. | Your numbers never come up and on retirement you realise that if you had invested the same amount each week in your super instead of lotto, you would now have generated more than $200 000 extra in your super account. |

# Chapter 6

## Where to from here — retirement and beyond

Retirement can be something we approach with anticipation or dread. In some cases it will be our financial preparedness or the strength of our desire to keep working or not that may drive these emotions.

Retirement can also sometimes feel like a one-way door, a step without the ability to go back into the workforce. This is somewhat dependent on how the retirement happened. For many people, taking a number of years to go from full-time work to retirement can make the transition less stressful.

In any event, we want to look at how to deal with financial shocks like that which occurred in 2008 while retired. The vast majority of retirees will feel that going back to work is not an option when something like this happens. We also need to get a handle on the extent of damage that such an event can cause and place it in perspective. Before we start looking at strategies for the aftermath of the Global Financial Crisis, it is worth reflecting on how we have got to this point and to truthfully and honestly look at what we need to do to manage the future.

## Understand the journey

Before we launch into strategies, you should revisit the journey you are trying to make. This means making sure that you know where you are now, where you are trying to get to, and how long you can take to get there.

For retirees, the journey is about lifestyle. The time for sacrificing current income in order to save for the future has past. While many retirees want to preserve capital, there comes a time where capital needs to be used in order to maintain lifestyle. You know how much your lifestyle costs. The question then becomes a simple one: will your financial resources last long enough if you maintain this lifestyle?

We can therefore reflect the success (or otherwise) of these strategies by comparing the length of time a specific cost of living will last given the available financial resources with a relevant life expectancy.

### Retirement resources

Most self funded retirees have a similar set of financial assets at their disposal:

- ⇨ Self funded pension account, such as an allocated pension or term pension. These are pension products that are based on an account balance that pays the owner an income stream until the pension account runs out of money. They are the most common form of pension used by self funded retirees.

- ⇨ Other investments, such as investment properties or shares and cash reserves.
- ⇨ Life pension. These are pensions that pay an income for the rest of the pension owner's life no matter how long the owner lives. These pensions are generally offered by either life insurance companies or by old corporate and public service superannuation schemes. They are not common anymore and can be quite expensive to purchase.
- ⇨ Age Pension. This is the pension provided by the government for all eligible Australians. Following changes introduced in 2006, the Age Pension is now more easily accessed as a part pension but it remains at a relatively low level compared to an average wage. The maximum Age Pension in the 2008/09 year is only \$24 414 for a couple and \$14 615 for a single pensioner. The 2009 Federal Budget announced modest increases to the maximum single Age Pension going up to \$16 504 per annum and the couple Age Pension to \$25 274 per annum combined. These amounts will be indexed from 20 September 2009. While this is a very small amount to live on, the access to part Age Pensions means that many self funded retirees can now access the Age Pension as a supplement to their other retirement resources.
- ⇨ Their home and other residential property. Many Australians have a large amount of personal wealth tied up in their home and have accrued the odd investment property throughout their lives. Increasingly, retirees will need to find ways to tap into that wealth.

- ⇨ Their family. Though many Australians would prefer not to become a 'burden to their family', children and grandchildren can become sources of help in the latter stages of retirement. This is especially true as both financial resources get used up and as physical assistance requirements escalate.

These resources are concrete to a degree. Another trait that you should look at is the concept of flexibility. If you launched into retirement with clear goals about how you would live and what you would leave behind for family, you may need to be flexible about some of these goals as circumstances change. The fact of the matter is that if you live longer than you expected then you will need to use up more of these resources than you may have originally planned.

## Age Pension

If you are not sure whether you can access the Age Pension or other social security benefits, or if you are concerned that you are not maximising your social security benefits, you should contact Centrelink. They have a good website that covers most of the basics in terms of entitlements and eligibility but you should be aware that it is complicated and some of the terms used on the website for various products aren't particularly intuitive. As an example, when looking at the income test for an Age Pension, superannuation-based pension products are described as 'asset test exempt income streams' or 'asset tested income streams (long term)' or 'asset tested income streams (short term)'.

Centrelink does offer free seminars on the Age Pension entitlements and application process, and these can be accessed via <www.centrelink.gov.au/internet/internet.nsf/services/fis_seminars.htm>. There is also free access to a financial information service (FIS) at <www.centrelink.gov.au/internet/internet.nsf/services/fis.htm>.

The FIS officers are available at various centres around the country specialising in retirement matters. You can make an appointment to have a free, one-on-one consultation. You don't have to be eligible for Centrelink assistance. The officers can help you determine your eligibility and help you maximise your benefits.

## Work out the gaps

Now that you have gathered together the basic information, you can start to do a realistic assessment of the adequacy of your retirement resources.

Throughout this book, you will see reference to the FIDO pension calculator at <www.fido.gov.au> as this calculator provides a good, easy-to-use tool that will help you see the impacts that the various strategies can have on your retirement outcomes. This is a service provided by the Australian Securities & Investments Commission.

The basic information you need to get going is:

- your current age
- your lifestyle cost
- the current balance of your pension or retirement products
- any other financial resources or assets that can be converted to an income stream
- your life expectancy (see chapter 2).

The FIDO term allocated pension calculator is a great tool to help with this. A term allocated pension is a retirement product that will pay out a reasonably stable income over a target time period. We can use this calculator to estimate how long an allocated pension will last given a starting balance and a particular level of income payments. Alternatively, you can use it to estimate how much an allocated pension will pay in income for a given starting balance and term.

The primary strategies that we will use are all designed to either extend the length of time that your resources will last, or to allow you to consider other resources that you may have access to but are not currently planning to use. We will also look at whether you are maximising your retirement income — in effect whether you are actually accessing all of the retirement income you can.

We will then run through a series of case studies that show how the strategies can work in real life situations.

## Strategy 1: choose your investment option

In the earlier chapters we have seen how important it is to choose wisely when it comes to investment options, because the right choice can make a big difference to the amount of superannuation accumulated. In your case the right investment choice can preserve your retirement resources for longer.

Almost all allocated retirement products offer you investment choice within that fund. Most funds will segment their investment options into one of six or so categories based on a risk versus return profile:

- *Cash:* 100 per cent invested in cash or similar securities.
- *Conservative:* Approximately 30 per cent invested in growth-style investments (Australian shares,

international shares and property) and 70 per cent invested in income-style investments (cash, Australian fixed interest or bonds and international fixed interest).

- ⇨ *Moderately conservative:* Approximately 50 per cent invested in growth-style investments and 50 per cent invested in income-style investments.
- ⇨ *Balanced:* Approximately 70 per cent invested in growth-style investments and 30 per cent invested in income-style investments.
- ⇨ *Growth:* Approximately 85 per cent invested in growth-style investments and 15 per cent invested in income-style investments.
- ⇨ *High growth:* Approximately 95 per cent invested in growth-style investments. Some small amounts of cash may exist as a result of cash flow requirements.

Funds differ in how they describe their options. Some funds will call 50 per cent growth/50 per cent income a balanced option, while other funds will call 70 per cent growth/30 per cent income a balanced option. The important thing is the amount of growth assets (shares or property) versus the amount of income or defensive assets (fixed interest and cash), rather than the name of the investment option. We have used the asset allocations shown above for all projections in this book.

The cash option will offer a low long-term return with low volatility (or risk). In contrast, the high-growth option will generally achieve the highest long-term return, however it will have higher volatility over shorter periods. The other options fall in between in terms of both return and volatility.

There is an important thing to note here and that is the word 'generally'. You can show data that reveals over a specific 10-year period some of the more conservative options outperform the high-growth options — the 10 years between 1 January 1999 and 31 December 2008 for example.

*Generally* the more growth assets your investments contain, the higher return you will receive over the long term. For projections we need to use an estimate of investment performance in the future. The projections used in our case studies use estimated future investment performance supplied by ASIC (as shown in table 6.1).

**Table 6.1: estimated future investment performance**

| Investment option | Estimate of future long-term (10+ years) investment performance before tax and fees |
|---|---|
| High-growth option (95% growth assets) | 9.0% pa |
| Growth option (85% growth assets) | 8.5% pa |
| Balanced option (70% growth assets) | 8.0% pa |
| Conservative option (35% growth assets) | 6.0% pa |
| Capital stable or cash (0% growth assets) | 5.5% pa |

*Source:* FIDO and Chant West.

The important part of this is to realise that the investment choices you make can make a very substantial difference to the end result you generate, but *only if you have time on your side*. For a retiree who has both a long life expectancy and sufficient assets to last over that long time frame, directing the bulk of investments into a balanced or growth option will almost certainly produce a higher chance of preserving capital and lifestyle than using a cash option. On the other hand, if you don't have time on your side then the upside of using a balanced or growth option may not be sufficient to offset the risk compared to the higher degree of certainty offered by a cash option.

Another interesting element to your investment choice occurs if you are eligible for a part Age Pension. The Age Pension income level can be reset as a result of changes in your other assets and income. If your allocated pension drops in value, you can ask for your Age Pension to be reassessed to take into account the new lower value of other assets and thereby increasing the Age Pension subject to age pension limits. This Age Pension resetting can help smooth the impacts of short-term volatility in the values of some of your other investments. As a result, you can use this to potentially take on slightly higher risk levels with your other investments.

## Strategy 2: accessing equity from residential property

In reviewing your retirement resources you may have recognised that an untapped resource is the value tied up in your residential property. If you have an investment property then clearly the easiest way to access that equity is to sell the property and reinvest the proceeds in such a way that an income stream can be generated. While investment properties do generate an income stream out of the rental return, these rental returns are often quite low as a percentage of the value of the property, and after all costs such as property maintenance and real estate agent fees are taken into account.

If the property in question is your home, you also need to consider how and where you will live as part of that equity access. In this case there are two main ways to access some of that value or equity:

- ⇨ Sell the home and either buy a cheaper property in which to live or become a long-term renter.
- ⇨ Take out a reverse mortgage.

## Sell the home

For many retirees, the prospect of selling their home would be a difficult and unhappy decision to make.

The pure finances of the transaction are relatively simple in that the proceeds of the sale of the home release a large amount of money to be used in other ways. Some of that money needs to be used for accommodation, either through long-term renting or via the purchase of a cheaper property to be used as the home going forward.

There are some reasonably significant financial considerations to take into account though. If you are a recipient of a part or full Age Pension then you need to understand the impact of the home sale on your Age Pension entitlement. Both the asset and income test will need to be recalculated based on your expectations of the new financial situation as a result of the home equity release.

The transaction costs of selling and buying real estate are quite high. There will be costs involved in preparing the property for sale, real estate agent commissions and legal costs. This can easily add up to 5 per cent of the value of the property or more depending upon the property preparation costs. In addition the purchase of the new property will involve more legal costs and possibly some home alterations to get the new, cheaper home into shape. On top of this you can also add the cost of the move and possible storage of furniture if the transition between homes cannot be done in one go.

By assuming that you will need to spend somewhere between $50 000 and $100 000 in transition costs between the existing home and the new, cheaper home, it becomes apparent that you will need to move to a substantially cheaper home before this becomes a worthwhile course of action. You then need to take into account whether such a move generates a hit to your lifestyle, and remember that it is lifestyle preservation that we are trying to achieve in the first place.

## Reverse mortgage

A reverse mortgage is basically a loan that is provided to you by a bank or mortgage provider. It differs from normal bank loans in that the bank does not expect you to make regular repayments of the loan. The bank secures the loan against the value of your home, on the basis that when you either move out of the home or die, the home will be sold and the bank loan will be repaid from the proceeds of the home sale.

The loan can be taken as either a lump-sum amount or as an income stream to replace or supplement your other retirement income sources. The most common loan is one where a series of small lump sums are taken. In this way you can manage the draw downs from the loan in such a way that you have sufficient money to live off, without significantly impacting any Age Pension entitlements that you would otherwise receive.

Reverse mortgages allow you to access some of the value of your home without the need to sell the home and bear all of those transaction costs. On the face of it, this sounds like a good, flexible way of accessing this equity and, used wisely, reverse mortgages can allow you to maintain lifestyle as other retirement resources start to run out.

As with everything though, there are some traps.

The interest rates that banks charge for reverse mortgages are generally around 1 per cent per annum higher than charged on a normal mortgage.

If the loan is taken out over a long time frame there is potential for the value of the loan to exceed the value of the house, which can create a situation called 'negative equity'. If this situation occurs, you or your estate will need to repay the additional loan amount, over and above the sale proceeds of the home. Some reverse mortgages have what is called a 'negative equity guarantee'. In these loans the lender guarantees that the maximum amount of money required to discharge the loan will be limited to the eventual sale proceeds of the house. However, this guarantee can be voided by the bank if they can prove that the house was not maintained to a standard that is set by the bank at the time the loan is taken out.

The maximum amount that you can borrow is usually set between 15 per cent and 40 per cent of the value of the property. The actual amount that you can borrow is dependent upon your age — the older you are the more you can borrow.

While these amounts sound low compared to the value of the house, compound interest can bite you here if the loan is taken out over a long time frame. Remember that while the home will generally increase in value over time, the long-term annual capital growth rate of residential real estate is around 3 per cent and generally lower than mortgage interest rate costs.

A maximum reverse mortgage loan of 40 per cent taken as a lump sum, where the reverse mortgage interest rate is 8 per cent and the capital growth on the property is assumed to be 3 per cent, means that you reach a point of negative equity in around 18 years. If the interest rate on the loan was 11 per cent per annum, you would reach this point in just 11 years.

The main advantage of reverse mortgages is that they allow you to access the value of the equity in your home while you live there. The main risk is the potential that you or your estate will wind up owing more than the home is worth when you move or die.

Like any risk, this can be managed. By following a few simple rules reverse mortgages can be a great way to access home equity:

1 Use reverse mortgages for income stream replacement rather than accessing a large lump sum at the start of the loan period.
2 Use reverse mortgages later in life when other non-debt resources have been used up.
3 Use a reverse mortgage with a negative equity guarantee.
4 Make sure you understand the fine print.
5 Get advice on the impacts to your Age Pension entitlements.

## Strategy 3: go on — have a red hot go!

Many people have difficulty in dealing with the certainty of life being finite — or more bluntly, the certainty that death will happen at some point. Some people also have difficulty with attempting to utilise all of their financial resources before they die.

Part of this may relate to generational differences in upbringing. If you are in your 70s or older, you grew up in an era that was very different to that of the next generation. Growing up in the 1930s and 1940s meant hardship and sacrifice for most, and it instilled a sense of frugality and saving for the future.

By way of contrast, the following generations seem to have a strong desire to utilise their assets for the preservation and maximisation of their own lifestyle.

Equally true for your generation is a strong desire to pass hard-earned assets on to children and grandchildren. For many people in this age group, residential real estate formed the basis of their retirement assets rather than superannuation. This has created a large number of people who are asset rich but income poor — technically millionaires but with lifestyles that are more consistent with struggling pensioners.

Another way to look at this is to consider that dying rich may be the ultimate in financial mismanagement. The idea of ensuring that you don't run out of money before you die seems to be entirely acceptable, whereas an attempt to make sure that you don't leave any money behind appears selfish and brings guilt. In reality, the latter is just a more refined version of the former.

## Strategy 4: get advice

No matter how good the websites, calculators, books (yes, even this one) and education seminars, personalised advice should be better. If the advice is coming from a qualified expert, with your best interests at heart, then there is no better way to get your own situation and needs fully explained and solutions explored. You can access financial advice through most superannuation and retirement funds these days, including industry funds.

There is an 'if' in that last paragraph that does need to be explored, and ultimately there are degrees within the quality of advice you can receive. Clearly, an adviser needs to be appropriately licensed and have relevant qualifications. Another good rule of thumb is to determine who is paying the adviser — you or someone else.

If you are in a retail pension fund then there is a good chance that you may be charged an adviser service fee each year. This will be shown on your annual statement if it is the case, along with contact details for your adviser. If you are being charged such a fee, it may be worthwhile talking to the adviser about your own situation and what sort of help he or she can provide you with for the service fee and how much extra it would cost to get more comprehensive advice.

Do your research though and ensure that if you do decide to get additional advice it is from someone appropriately qualified and that the advice won't be conflicted via commissions received for recommending certain products. At the end of the day you should feel happy to pay the adviser for his or her services rather than get a 'free' or heavily discounted service because the products that the adviser will place you in pay the adviser a commission. By making sure that you pay the adviser, you can have comfort that you will be told the best things for you to do, even if it doesn't involve an investment.

An adviser can also help with your broader investment needs and should be able to advise on not only your retirement funds in terms of all of the strategies mentioned here, but also on Age Pension entitlements and reverse mortgage products.

We look in more detail at how to get advice the right way in chapter 7.

For many retirees, 2008 was a year that generated enormous concern and sense of personal financial loss. Part of this sense of loss was compounded by news and media stories that headline with massive losses for the superannuation industry and a focus on the negative returns generated for pure sharemarket investments.

Most retirees use a balanced option, and on average these options lost around 22 per cent during 2008. The headlines tend to ignore the fact that these same investment options returned over 13 per cent per annum on average over the previous four years leading up to 2008. In addition, the five-year annual return for these options was 5.3 per cent per annum — marginally better than cash options for the same period and a respectable return given that one of the five years was a once-in-100-years shocker.

In addition, many retirees don't think about the enormous amount of personal wealth that may be tied up in their family home. There are tools and strategies that can help you access that wealth without necessarily impacting on your enjoyment of living in the home.

The important things to take out of this are to focus on where you are now, incorporate all of your assets within your planning, understand the impact or sensitivity that your decisions around investment changes will make, and always refer the potential outcomes back to the core goals of maintaining lifestyle.

## Case study — Tony and Margaret

Tony is a male aged 75 at 2008. He is married to Margaret, who is aged 72, and they currently have a lifestyle that costs them $50 000 a year.

Tony and Margaret have $300 000 left in their allocated pension accounts. They own their own home in Sydney which is worth approximately $800 000 and they receive a part Age Pension of $18 000 a year combined. This means that they are drawing down on their allocated pension at the rate of $32 000 a year.

Tony and Margaret are active people and are not overweight. While they enjoy a regular glass of wine with meals, they have never smoked and are in general good health.

The average life expectancy in Australia for a male aged 75 is 10.9 years. For a female it is 15.5 years. It is worth remembering that this does not represent a prediction that a 75-year-old male in average health will live for 10.9 years. Rather, it is saying that for all 75-year-old males, the average number of years they will live will be 10.9 years. Because the distribution of all of those lives will be normal, you can also say that roughly half will live for less than 10.9 years and half will live for longer.

Given that Tony and Margaret are both relatively fit, active and have never smoked, we can say that they have a good chance of living longer than the average. If we add five years to the longer of the two average life expectancies we can work out a conservative estimate of how long we need to make their retirement resources last — let's call it 20 years.

According to the FIDO term pension calculator, using a term of 20 years with an opening balance of $300 000 and all other calculator parameters left in default mode, Tony and Margaret can expect to generate an income of $21 600 per annum if they want their allocated pension to last the full 20 years. This income will be adjusted for inflation as well.

Alarmingly this is well short of the $32 000 a year that they are currently drawing out of the allocated pension products. If they continue to spend the $32 000 per annum, their allocated pension will run out in about 12 years.

Clearly Tony and Margaret have a funding gap in their retirement plans. If they do nothing different their allocated pensions will run out well before their death. When their allocated pensions do run out they may suffer a very serious lifestyle reduction. We need to try to help them bridge this gap.

## Tony and Margaret choose their investment option (strategy 1)

They don't have the ability, opportunity or desire to go back to work at this stage of their lives and try to fill the gap with a new employment income. Nor can they completely plug this gap by taking on a higher risk investment option.

Even though they are in their mid 70s, their circumstances mean that their retirement resources may need to last another 20 years. Despite this, their current lifestyle will use up their allocated resources much quicker, and given the shorter time frame a riskier investment strategy may not be warranted. Given the very poor performance of the investment markets in 2008, they are thinking seriously about switching all of their remaining allocated pension assets into cash.

During the years of their retirement so far, they have used a common retirement strategy of holding the next two years of allocated pension draw downs in the cash option and the remainder of their allocated pension in the balanced option. During 2008 they have used up the money in the cash option and have not made a switch out of the balanced option to replenish the cash account, hoping that the investment markets recover before they need to use any of the money in the balanced option. They have sufficient money left in the cash option to get them through 2009 but will have to then switch money from the balanced option for 2010 draw downs.

This strategy of keeping the bulk of their allocated pension assets in a balanced option should allow their allocated pensions to run out in 12 years, assuming that the balanced option delivers them an 8 per cent return before management fees. If Tony and Margaret switch all of the allocated pension assets to the cash option which would return an estimated 5.5 per cent before fees, they should expect that their allocated pensions will run out after about 10 years rather than 12. While this is not a big difference, it is an approach that potentially adds to the gap rather than diminishes it.

Tony and Margaret have also reflected on the fact that they have been retired since Tony turned 60 in 1993. Since then they have lived through the 1994 Bond Market Collapse, the 1997 Asian Currency Crisis, the 1998 Russian Bond Crisis and the 2001 Tech Wreck. In each of these previous sharemarket crises, they have stuck to their strategy of holding a bit in cash and leaving the rest in a balanced option.

The investment performance of their balanced option throughout the 16 years to the end of 2008 was 8.4 per cent per annum compound. This includes –22.2 per cent for the 2008 year. This is based on the average performance achieved by a 70 per cent growth/30 per cent defensive portfolio for the 16 years in an allocated pension, before fees and tax.

So Tony and Margaret have a difficult decision. On the one hand they have enjoyed the benefits delivered by a good strategy that has worked well over the long term, even when it includes a once-in-100-years period of poor performance. On the other hand, they recognise that the sharemarkets remain very volatile and unstable and they have now reached a stage where their allocated pension has only a limited time left in any event. For them the uncertainty of the sharemarkets coupled with the shorter term of their investments offsets the potential gain from a potential market recovery.

As a result, Tony and Margaret have decided to accept their losses over the last year, and switch all of their remaining allocated pension assets into the cash investment option. This means that they will not benefit from any market recovery, but they protect themselves from further losses if the recovery does not occur for some time.

Our projections now estimate that their allocated pension income will run out 10 years too soon.

## Tony and Margaret access equity in their property (strategy 2)

Tony and Margaret don't have the ability, opportunity or desire to go back to work at this stage of their lives and try to fill the gap with a new employment income. Nor can they realistically plug this gap by taking on a higher risk investment option. They therefore decide that they will plan to use the equity in their home once the allocated pension runs out.

Let's fast forward 10 years to 2019.

Margaret is now 82, and while still quite sprightly is starting to suffer from many of the ailments affecting people in their later years. Tony is now 85, and to be blunt is on his last legs. He is reasonably dependent on others and they have realised that Margaret can no longer cope by herself, with the issues of looking after him.

They both desperately want to stay in their own home and live out their remaining years there. A realistic and difficult discussion with their doctor has made them realise that Tony probably has no more than two years left, but Margaret can expect to live for another eight to 10 years.

Their allocated pensions are about to run out. They know that their income will drop significantly by the end of the year when the last draw down from their allocated pension is made, despite the fact that they will then be entitled to a full Age Pension.

Their home is now worth $1.1 million, and their current lifestyle costs — while the same as 10 years ago in real terms — are now at $67 000 per annum. The maximum Age Pension for a couple is now worth $33 000 per annum.

The additional aged care services that they will need to use to help keep Tony in the home will cost them about $30 000 a year for the next two years. This means that their income requirements to maintain their lifestyle will be $97 000 per annum for the next two years and then $67 000 per annum for the following eight years. After allowance for a full Age Pension, the income gap will be $64 000 per annum for the next two years and $34 000 per annum for the eight years after that, with all amounts indexed to inflation.

Given that a core aspect of their lifestyle preservation is to continue to live in their current home, they are not considering selling the home and moving to a cheaper one. Instead they are looking at taking out a reverse mortgage on their home.

Tony and Margaret have found a reverse mortgage with an interest rate of 8 per cent per annum. For the purposes of planning, they assume that their home value will increase at 3 per cent per annum—broadly in line with inflation. By the year 2029, after taking out all of their income gap requirements as described above, Margaret will owe around $650 000, but her home will be worth around $1.48 million, leaving her with remaining home equity of around $830 000. These numbers are in 2029 dollars, which are worth $460 000 in 2009 dollars assuming inflation of 3 per cent per annum.

In this way, Tony and Margaret have successfully managed to maintain a lifestyle based on $50 000 per annum indexed for around 20 years after the 2008 global sharemarket collapse. They have achieved this goal while reducing their risk.

Their primary assets at the start of that 20-year period were a $300 000 allocated pension and a home worth $800 000. They have intelligently used their superannuation assets in conjunction with the Age Pension and then managed to extract an income out of the value of their home without selling the home. They have even been able to manage to leave an estate worth nearly $460 000 in today's dollars to their family.

## Case study — Aldo and Anna

During his working years Aldo built a successful business based on a chain of hardware stores in Melbourne. He sold this business in 1999 when he and Anna were both 50 years old. By the end of 2003 he had drip fed the proceeds into superannuation accounts for both himself and Anna, and at that stage the superannuation accounts were worth $1 million in total. They are relatively conservative investors and use a balanced investment option. They also have a nice home in Melbourne.

For the next four years their superannuation investments enjoyed a great ride — the average balanced option investment return after fees and tax was 13.6 per cent per annum — and by the end of 2007, their superannuation investments were worth $1.67 million. During 2008 they watched with mounting horror as their superannuation account balances lost 22 per cent of their value. Their superannuation balances at the end of 2008 were worth $1.3 million. In one year they had watched nearly $370 000 get wiped off their superannuation account balances.

During their regular review of their financial situation, their financial adviser asked them to consider the long-term performance of their super investments. Over the five years since 2003, their superannuation accounts had actually earned a compound annual return of 5.3 per cent per annum after fees and taxes. The cash option in their superannuation fund had returned only 4.5 per cent per annum over the same five years. Even though this five-year period included a once-in-100-years horror story for investment markets, their strategy of using a balanced option had still delivered a compound investment return that was better than cash over that five years.

Now at age 60 Aldo and Anna were looking at what they should do in terms of the next stage of their retirement. This would mean transferring their superannuation assets to some allocated pensions. Their lifestyle costs them around $80 000 per annum. Their superannuation accounts mean that they are not eligible for the Age Pension.

## Aldo and Anna choose their investment option (strategy 1)

Anna has the longer life expectancy of 26 years. The FIDO term allocated pension calculator estimates that their $1.3 million in allocated pensions will allow them to have an average income of $79 500 per annum indexed and after tax over 26 years, if they leave the bulk of their allocated pension assets invested in a balanced option. This strategy clearly allows them to maintain their lifestyle.

Despite feeling somewhat comforted by their adviser's information on the five-year earnings performance of their superannuation accounts, they asked their adviser what they could expect if they changed their investments to a cash option. Using the FIDO pension calculator again, we can see that if they maintain their current lifestyle, they would expect their allocated pension to run out in around 21 years. Alternatively, they could keep the pension going for the full 26 years of their plan by reducing their retirement income to $68 000 per annum indexed—a 15 per cent reduction in income. In effect, the cash option—while safeguarding them from future negative returns—actually guarantees them either a reduced lifestyle in retirement or that their allocated pensions will run out earlier than planned.

Given the long time frames involved, they decide to stick with a balanced investment option for their allocated pension.

## Aldo and Anna access equity in their property and have a red hot go (strategies 2 and 3)!

Aldo and Anna also have the opportunity to enhance their lifestyle. We have already seen that provided Aldo and Anna maintain their balanced investment strategy, our projections indicate that they will be able to maintain their current lifestyle — which costs around $80 000 a year — by just using their allocated pensions.

Their home in Melbourne is now worth $1 million and they are wondering what sort of lifestyle they could achieve if they also accessed some of the value tied up in their home. If we attempt to maximise the income achievable out of their allocated pensions and home over 26 years (Anna's life expectancy), what would that income look like?

We can do this in a fairly conservative way by maintaining the allocated pension money in the balanced option and by reducing the time that the allocated pensions need to run, thereby increasing the income stream that the pensions pay. This will of course mean that the allocated pensions run out before the 26-year mark, but we can then look at replacing that income with a reverse mortgage once the pensions run out.

A conservative approach to using reverse mortgages is to aim for a total debt at the end of the reverse mortgage of less than 50 per cent of the value of the home. We have also assumed that the home value will increase by only 3 per cent per annum and that the interest rate on the reverse mortgage will be 8 per cent per annum.

Doing the maths reveals that Aldo and Anna could plan a lifestyle cost of around $91 000 a year indexed at 3 per cent per annum using this technique—a 14 per cent improvement in retirement income. The allocated pensions would last approximately 21 years, and then the reverse mortgage would take over for the next five years. At the end of the full 26-year period the home would be worth $2.2 million and the reverse mortgage debt would be $1.1 million, leaving home equity of $1.1 million which is around $500 000 in today's dollars.

There are a number of assumptions that affect these results. Things that could cause a problem for the projections are:

- ⇨ Either Aldo or Anna live longer than 26 years.
- ⇨ The investment returns on the allocated pensions wind up being less than 8 per cent per annum.
- ⇨ The capital growth on the house is less than 3 per cent per annum.
- ⇨ The reverse mortgage rate for the last five years of the 26-year period is higher than 8 per cent per annum.

Equally, the reality may be that some of these numbers go in the opposite direction, making the results more favourable to Aldo and Anna. The strategy can be refined over the years though—it does not have to be set in concrete on day one. As time goes by all of the assumptions can be tested for validity and changed to reflect the best available information.

The point is to consider all of your assets when planning your retirement, and especially try to include one of the biggest—your home.

## Case study—Frida

Frida is 80 years old and her husband George died of a heart attack three years ago. She has a home in the western suburbs of Sydney worth $600 000 and six investment properties with no debt, scattered throughout various suburbs of Sydney. These properties in total are worth $2 million and provide a gross rental income of $60 000 a year. George's term allocated pension reverted into her name on his death and pays her an income of $15 000 a year.

## Frida chooses her investment option (strategy 1)

As Frida's remaining allocated pension is quite small and as she is now 80 years old, she is using the cash investment option for her allocated pension. She will gain very little advantage by changing this to a higher risk option given the low remaining balances and short time frames involved, so she maintains her allocated pension in the cash option.

## Frida accesses equity from her property (strategy 2)

Frida's home is worth around $600 000. This could well be an asset that she will decide to use in the future, but she also has the six investment properties to consider.

While the residential investments are paying what appears to be a reasonable rental return, the properties are quite old and are requiring a fair amount of maintenance. On average she is spending around $5000 a year per property on maintenance and upkeep. She uses a trusted real estate agent to manage the rental contracts at a standard rental income commission of 7 per cent. The combination of maintenance costs and agent fees means that her net income from the rental properties is only $26 000 per annum, giving her a total after-tax income of $35 000 per annum including the allocated pension income. Due to the extensive assets, Frida is not eligible for the Age Pension.

Her total assets—including her home, investment properties and allocated pension—are around $3 million, and yet her after-tax income is just over 1 per cent of that amount. She struggles to make ends meet and lives in virtual poverty compared to many of her friends.

She is considering selling some of the investment properties but is concerned that this will mean that she won't be able to leave a substantial estate to her two children, both of whom are in their 40s and are comfortably able to look after their own financial affairs.

Eventually she sits down with her children and has a full and frank discussion with them about her lifestyle. Her children strongly encourage her to restructure her assets so that she has greater access to the value. She decides to sell the properties that have the highest cost-to-income numbers, and in so doing releases $1.3 million of assets into cash. All of the properties in question were purchased before 20 September 1985 and no capital gains tax applies to the sales. Given that she is 80 years old and not working, Frida cannot get this money into the superannuation system.

She then decides to invest the proceeds in a simple and easy-to-implement strategy of holding $300 000 in a cash management trust and the remainder in a managed fund investment using a balanced investment option. Every year or so she will replenish the cash management trust assets out of the managed fund.

Eighty-year-old females in Australia have a life expectancy of 10 years, and as she feels healthy and active she has decided to manage her affairs on the basis that she will live for another 15 years. Thanks to the support from her children, she has decided to make the most of this time still available to her and to enhance her lifestyle to one that will cost around

$100 000 per annum after tax — a tripling in lifestyle cost but one that is totally within her means.

Frida will now travel as much as she can over the next few years. She plans to take one child with her on each of these trips. She has also decided to make sure that she spends as much time as she can with her family, but in a very enjoyable way, and plans to take the entire family out to the best restaurant she knows on a monthly basis.

Her children are delighted with these new arrangements. They had been concerned under the old arrangements as her very poor income had not only been obviously problematic for Frida, it also meant that she was unable to afford basic maintenance on her house and her children had been having to provide a lot of these basic maintenance services. The changes mean that she can now afford to outsource all of the maintenance issues of the remaining houses to qualified tradespeople. In addition, the time she will now spend with her children and their families will be of a much higher quality and much more enjoyable for all.

## The next step

The strategies outlined in this chapter are largely about getting better control over your pension and really understanding how all of your retirement resources can be harnessed to give you the best possible retirement income. The next steps are:

1. Gather information on all of your retirement resources, including your property, and make sure that you are maximising your social security benefits.
2. Choose your investment strategy — be prepared to reduce risk if either your own life expectancy or the

remaining investment assets mean that you don't have a long time frame to consider.

3 Access equity tied up in residential properties — investment properties can have low net income yields and your own house is a resource that can be used even while you are living in it.
4 Think about getting financial advice.
5 Read the next chapters to see how you can add further protection to your retirement resources.

# Chapter 7

## Don't lose it again

A natural reaction to an event or situation that causes you pain is to try to ease that pain. If you hold your hand over a naked flame from a candle there is a reasonable chance that you will either remove the hand or suffer painful burns.

The same rules apply to your finances. An event or situation that causes you to lose money will naturally be avoided in the future. Sometimes the hard thing is to determine what has actually caused the losses. Is it the fact that you were an investor during 2008, or was it the fact that world markets went through a once-in-a-lifetime sharemarket collapse? Blaming the financial losses on yourself for being an investor during 2008 is a bit like blaming the pain from the candle burn on having a hand.

There are things that will help you get your finances back in shape, but deciding to not invest again is not one of those things. As superannuation is such a long-term investment, you can afford to ride out the ups and downs and not worry too much about the short-term pain. That said, it is worth reviewing your superannuation just as you would any other investment.

## Reviewing your investments

As with any long-range plan, it makes sense to have a regular review process in place. Investment reviews should be no different to any other business or commercial project review.

There should be an appropriate review schedule in place, one that doesn't happen so often as to be meaningless, but does allow you to make sure that major milestones are being achieved. The reviews should always go back to test the progress against the core issues of your investment strategy — the goals, time frames and risk appetite. Likewise, you should also look to do a major review if one of these core issues within the financial plan has changed.

In chapters 4 and 5 you would have seen some strategies on banking the winnings. During the times that the sharemarkets are booming, a review of your investments — which properly references your investment plan and how you are tracking towards your goals — may indicate that you are actually ahead of plan. During these times it may be worthwhile working out how much of your investments can be de-risked or moved into a lower volatility, lower returning asset class while still allowing you to reach your goals.

## The wrong reasons for investment decisions

Just as it is important to review your investments for the right reasons, it can be argued that it is equally important to not do it for the wrong reasons. In fact, if you do chop and change your investments based on the wrong reasons there is a good chance you will be committing one of the cardinal sins of long-term investment — tinkering. Some of the worst things to act on are worth describing in a bit of detail.

### *Fear and greed*

The fear and greed cycle drives this illogical behaviour, and unfortunately it is a powerful cycle as the process of ignoring it requires us to ignore a lot of the inputs we are getting from other sources.

Interestingly, this cycle is a classic example of the whole being greater than the sum of the parts. Investing in greedy stages of the cycle is still okay provided that the investments are then held long term; in other words, if the fear stage of the cycle is ignored. It is when the full cycle operates that real damage can be done to an investment portfolio as this cycle encourages you to invest in the greed-driven expensive stages and sell out in the fear-driven discounted stages.

The other important part of this is to acknowledge that a transfer of long-term wealth often occurs during these volatile and uncertain periods. For all of the investors who are driven by the fear and greed cycle, there are usually a much smaller number who invest based on logical fundamentals. These few happily purchase the assets of the many when they are cheap, and willingly sell assets when they are being highly sought after and expensive. The result is a direct transfer of wealth from the impatient to the patient.

Dealing with the fear and greed cycle does not require you to be an active investor—such a person is someone who actively purchases and sells investments, whereas a passive investor purchases investments and then holds them for the long term. Clearly, buying investments as they become expensive and selling them as they become cheap is fundamentally flawed from a logical perspective, but buying investments when they are cheap and selling them when they are expensive, while logical, requires that you have a process of valuing investments that can accurately describe an investment as either 'cheap' or 'expensive'.

This is much more difficult than it sounds when you are attempting to do it in real time. Even some of the best investment minds in the world get this wrong.

Warren Buffett is widely regarded as one of the best share-market investors of our time. On 23 September 2008 he made a US$5 billion investment in Goldman Sachs, one of the US's largest financial services businesses. At the time of the investment, Goldman Sachs was trading at around US$125 per share. Goldman Sachs had reached a maximum closing price of nearly US$248 just 11 months before in October 2007, and so US$125 per share looked cheap. Within two months of that purchase though, the share price had fallen to US$52, creating an on-paper loss of nearly US$3 billion for Mr Buffett.

While this sounds like a horrendous result, it has to be taken into the context of the time frame of the investment. If Mr Buffett's investment time frame is five to 10 years then this could still prove to be a very good investment, even though with the benefit of a perfect cheapness 'predictor'—which doesn't exist—it would have been even better if he had delayed the purchase by a couple of months.

If you do not possess a process of constant and accurate valuation of investments, as a long-term investor you should try to ignore any active investing process and simply rely on holding investments for the long term and purchasing more investments on a regular basis.

## *The media and what (not) to believe*

In many ways it is unfair to blame the media for driving fear and greed cycles. After all, the content that we get through our media is usually a reflection of what we want to hear about. Weekly magazines wouldn't bother to constantly print speculation about Hollywood stars if we didn't want to read about it. Similarly, headlines about catastrophic sharemarket meltdowns wouldn't appear if we didn't lap this sort of stuff up.

We as media consumers must therefore take some responsibility for the way investment information is presented, and if we start to be discerning about this information and where we get it from we should start to receive more balanced information.

Importantly, the TV and daily paper news media are built on the events of the day. Getting commentary that takes into account long-term trends and events is pretty much outside the realm of reporting for daily-based news media. Long-term trends therefore are more the realm of analysis, and are perhaps best sought from dedicated financial news sites and sources.

Daily news also competes with itself. All major TV networks have news and current affairs programs, and all are advertising to potential viewers throughout the day. In a world where attention spans are shrinking and where a TV show advertisement only airs for 15 seconds, it is all about grabbing attention and headlines. Which of the following two promotional advertisements for a current affairs program do you think would generate the most viewers?

> *Tonight, learn how the sharemarket can slowly create wealth over the next 20 years.*
>
> *Tonight we show how pensioners' life savings have been wiped out by the greed of high-flying bankers.*

It is easy to work out which of these two would attract the higher number of viewers, and as a result which of the two stories would be aired. Equally clearly, you can see which of the two would generate the best long-term educational value to the viewing public.

## *Share price indices versus accumulation indices*

One of the other issues that we have with the majority of regular financial reporting is that the statistics that are often used are not the most appropriate statistics for superannuation investors. The All Ordinaries index is a good example — or any world sharemarket price index.

Most financial news tracks the relevant sharemarket *price* index to show trends in the markets around the world. Price indices show the movements in the prices of the shares. These indices effectively ignore the value of dividends that the underlying companies pay to their investors. Concentrating on a share price index is a bit like someone who analyses the return from an investment property but ignores the rental income and only looks at the capital gain on the property.

Company dividends are especially relevant to superannuation investors as these investors generally stay invested for long periods. The dividends generated within superannuation investment portfolios are reinvested with the company that paid the dividend, so the dividends become a significant part of the return for these investors. This is an important part of why compound interest works so well in superannuation.

To put the difference in perspective, consider figure 7.1, which shows both the Australian All Ordinaries share price index and the Accumulation index—the latter includes the dividends which are assumed to be reinvested. As you can see, over a long time frame the two indices look very different.

**Figure 7.1: All Ordinaries share price index and Accumulation index**

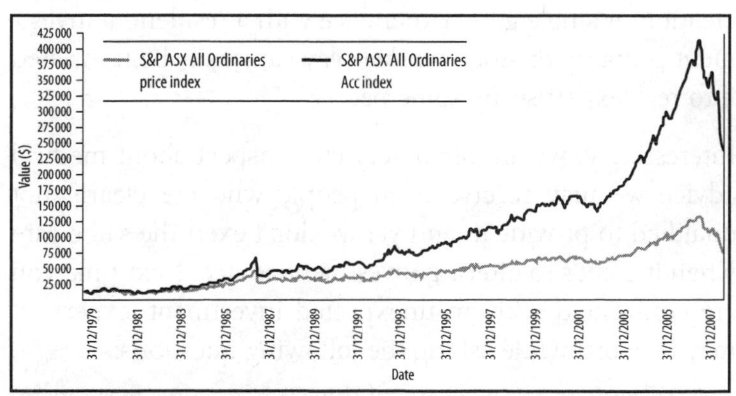


*Source:* Colonial First State.
Value of $10 000 invested at 31/12/1979 to 31/12/2008—S&P/ASX All Ordinaries price index vs S&P/ASX All Ordinaries Accumulation index.

## *Advice from non-qualified people*

Wealth for most of us is a subject worth discussing. Our interest in wealth starts at a very early age—small children have a concept of money and its role in the attainment of things from as young as three years old.

As our own wealth builds, as our aspirations increase and as we plan our lives we realise that almost every aspect of planning and goals we set for ourselves requires some additional element of wealth. With these underlying motivators, it is no surprise that wealth creation ideas are abundant.

Equally abundant are the sources of these wealth creation ideas. Parents, friends and the ubiquitous cab driver all have views on how to go about investing. In fact, what is rare is someone who *doesn't* have a view on how to build wealth.

If you really dig though, it becomes clear pretty quickly that most people have only limited experience on wealth creation. A single good experience with a residential investment property or stock market play can easily be translated into real 'expertise' by some people.

Interestingly, we are often very circumspect about medical advice we may receive from people who are clearly not qualified to provide it, and yet we don't exert the same care when it comes to filtering investment advice. Next time you are confronted with an unexpected investment 'expert', it may be worthwhile asking the following questions:

- ⇨ What is the real return of this strategy after fees, costs and taxes?
- ⇨ What does this return equate to on a per annum compound basis?
- ⇨ How does this return compare to alternative investment strategies?
- ⇨ Does this strategy apply across all time frames and investment cycles?

- ⇨ What is your approach to advising others in terms of understanding their investment needs?
- ⇨ Do you have appropriate qualifications and licences to give advice?

Another good test is to compare the cost of the advice to the probable value — free investment advice is often worth nothing.

Real expertise comes with broad knowledge of investment markets and processes. It requires significant investment in training and modelling systems. Just as important, a good financial planner must have the ability to listen, translate and develop appropriate wealth creation strategies that take into account the different needs of the individual clients.

### *Emotional responses*

The common thread of the previous sections can be described as 'bad information' and 'encouragement to do the illogical'.

The reason that these spurious inputs work on many people is that the inputs play to people's emotions. They are inputs that work because they push emotive buttons. Fear and greed play to the herd instincts of flight and safety in numbers. Media stories are often about hardship and disaster rather than slow success. Advice from non-qualified people is often framed around something that appears to be quick and easy. The emotional responses that these inputs trigger will generally lead to the same set of actions — realising losses by buying expensive investments and then selling them when they are cheaper.

The alternative wealth creation strategy of getting wealthy slowly but surely doesn't generate much in the way of emotional response — either positive or negative. Let's face it — such a strategy is pretty dull. At the end of the day though, a strategy of building wealth slowly and surely, using simple rules that work over defined long-term time frames and all stages of the investment cycle, actually has a much greater chance of success.

## Getting advice — the right way

Just as we have discussed the problems of getting inappropriate investment advice, it is worth reviewing the importance of getting quality investment advice.

The starting point for finding a financial planner is to first make sure that you haven't already got one. While this is a bit like saying in order to find a spouse you should first check whether you are not already married, the reason for the comment is that many people have a relationship with a financial planner or access to a panel of financial planners through their superannuation fund.

A simple check of your last superannuation fund statement or your superannuation fund's website or a call to the fund's client service call centre is a good way of determining whether you have access to a financial planner. Remember that if you have a retail or small employer superannuation arrangement, there is a good chance that you may already be paying a financial advice service fee, so it is important to ensure that you are getting full value for this service.

The next thing to consider is what type of advice you need. Is it limited advice in respect of just your superannuation, or is it a full financial plan that will look at all of your financial goals?

The former will usually be limited to advice on how to use your superannuation fund better. It may include advice on choosing investment options within the fund, life insurance needs and consolidation of other superannuation funds.

A full financial plan should take into account all of your financial assets and risk management, including your superannuation, your own home and other assets. A full financial plan should also explore a diverse range of wealth creation strategies, including how to use debt and home equity. It should be customised to your own circumstances and take into account such things as not only your pre- and post-retirement needs but also funding for things like education for children and estate planning. Risk management planning will include your and your partner's life insurance, income insurance as well as trauma and disability insurance, and even some aspects of general insurance needs.

The Financial Planning Association of Australia (FPA) has several helpful hints on their website that can show you how to find a financial planner and how to interview a planner to make sure that this person is right for you. Go to <www.fpa.asn.au>.

The 'find a planner' section allows you to search by both location and qualifications. The 'questions to ask a planner' section covers things like experience, qualifications, licensing and the process of payment for services, and importantly provides you with guidance as to appropriate answers to some of these questions. There is also a good section that shows the value of quality financial advice.

You should pay close attention to the payment options with a planner before you complete any agreement for services. The financial planning profession was built on a combination of sales and advice for the insurance and wealth management industry. The sales role meant that many planners received commissions from insurers and wealth managers rather than just fees from the people for whom they were providing the advice.

Over time, the financial planning industry has reshaped itself to be more focused on advice and less on sales, however a variety of commission- and fee-sharing models still exist. It is important to note where the advisers' incentives lie. Many advisers charge a fee based on the extent of the assets that they help you to manage. The idea is that the adviser's fee goes up as your wealth increases, so that the adviser is incentivised to work for your investment success.

Financial planning is a service that is worth having and therefore worth paying for. Important consideration should go into ensuring that you as the client are paying for the service. If any of your financial planner's income is going to come in the form of commissions from the products that the planner advises you to use, a legitimate question for you to ask is whether the advice you will receive will be biased because of those payments.

Even if the commission is structured in such a way that there is no bias towards one product provider compared to another, does the reliance on commission mean that the adviser is less likely to advise you to do things that don't generate a commission at all—such as pay off your non-deductible debt on your home, or take out more life insurance through your superannuation fund? Service agreements with financial advisers can now be structured in such a way that these questions can be appropriately answered.

There has been a lot of commentary about conflicts of interest within the financial planning industry. Some of this commentary is valid and has led to significant improvement in practices and payment for services.

It is worth noting that conflicts exist in almost every service industry. In many cases we are so accustomed to the conflicts that they are completely ignored. For example, doctors are paid by patients for medical treatment. The financial incentives here on the face of it would encourage the doctor to not cure the patient and to extend the treatment, because that would generate the best short-term financial outcome for the doctor. We know that such a thing would actually be very rare, and we as consumers of medical services are entirely comfortable with this potential conflict of interest.

The underlying message is that quality financial advice can be very worthwhile, but ensure that you are paying for it and that conflicts of interest are either removed or demonstrably dealt with to your satisfaction.

# Chapter 8

## Generating retirement income

The core of any plan that is intended to deliver financial security in retirement is simply putting aside a portion of your current income so that you can build a nest egg that is sufficient to draw down an income during retirement—during a time when income is not being earned through personal labour.

For most of us, the process of generating such a nest egg requires us to have a plan. A very small number of us will not need a plan. These few will either win a lottery, develop and sell a very successful business, inherit or have access to significant family wealth or have an exceptional earning capacity over a long period of time. For the rest, we will need to develop a carefully considered plan that will probably take decades to run. We will need to use investments like superannuation to achieve our financial security.

Uncertainty is a cornerstone of the investment process in that the more uncertain we are about the result of an investment opportunity, the higher the potential return we require to invest in that opportunity. Cash provides a relatively low return but with a high degree of certainty. The return from shares on the other hand is much more uncertain, and as a result we as investors require a higher return to compensate for that uncertainty.

Another thing to keep in mind when considering risk is to understand that a series of good years can have a double whammy effect on how we deal with and treat risk.

Investment managers and asset consultants are the professionals that often advise superannuation trustees on the fund investment options. Asset consultants think about risk as a deviation from the expected result. For them a higher than expected return is just as important to note and think about as a lower than expected number. A series of years that have delivered higher than expected returns may indicate that an investment bubble is building, and as a general rule bubbles tend to burst. Equally, a few years where returns have been lower than expected may mean that the prices for shares are becoming discounted below their true long-term value and represent bargain opportunities.

Investors on the other hand tend to think about risk just in terms of loss. They often only worry about the years where a bad result occurs and ignore the pressure that a series of good years places on market valuations. The compounding aspect of this is that a series of good years also builds expectations for investors. The market will be experiencing pressure because of more and more expensive share prices at the same time that our expectations are for continuing higher (than normal) investment returns.

When the bubble bursts, is it any wonder that we run for cover?

History shows that when investment market prices drift a long way from long-term investment averages, the swings in performance that follow can be very dramatic.

Table 8.1 highlights this. You will see that for each of the last four major sharemarket meltdown years, the preceding four years generally offered strong investment returns, and importantly, the four years that followed each of these bear markets were also strong ones.

**Table 8.1: negative return years from 1990 to 2008**

| Negative return years | Return (%) | Previous four years (% pa) | Previous four years (% cumulative) | Following four years (% pa) | Following four years (% cumulative) |
|---|---|---|---|---|---|
| 1990 | −4.6 | 18.4 | 96.6 | 11.8 | 56.4 |
| 1994 | −5.6 | 12.1 | 58.0 | 16.9 | 87.0 |
| 2002 | −6.8 | 8.9 | 40.5 | 14.5 | 71.8 |
| 2008 | −22.2 | 13.6 | 66.5 | ? | ? |

*Source:* Russell Investments.
*Note:* Returns are gross of fees and tax and based on indicative asset allocations.
Chant West Research Paper: Risk is a feeling, not a formula (February 2009).

## Risk management

In most situations we don't know what the return will be from a particular investment. We manage that uncertainty through basic—you might even say intuitive—risk management techniques. Our primary risk management techniques include avoidance of unnecessary risk and diversification of risk. By using these techniques well, we minimise the overall risk that we take on.

## Avoiding unnecessary risk

Avoiding unnecessary risk starts with the premise that for two different investments that promise the same potential return, we will intuitively use the investment option that has the lower risk—the investment that has more certainty of delivering the required result.

Based on returns actually achieved over the long term, Chant West estimates that the different types of investments (or asset classes) are most likely to provide the long-term (10 plus years) returns before fees and taxes shown in table 8.2.

**Table 8.2: long-term returns**

| | |
|---|---|
| Inflation | 3.0% pa |
| Cash | 5.5% pa |
| Fixed interest or bonds | 6.0% pa |
| Property | 7.5% pa |
| Shares | 9.5% pa |

*Source:* Chant West *Multi-Manager Quarterly*, December 2008, Vol. 6, No. 4, with data from Russell Investments.

This process of avoiding unnecessary risk also extends to not using investments that have no chance of delivering a required return. If you need your superannuation fund to achieve a return of, say, 8 per cent per annum after fees and taxes over 20 years in order to meet your goals then you clearly need to use investment options that can achieve such returns. If you just used cash in this situation you are virtually guaranteeing failure of achieving the required return of 8 per cent per annum.

## Diversification of risk

Once we have identified a universe of potential investments, a prudent investor will understand that the individual investment opportunities within that universe could deliver a return within a broad spectrum. An investment in a single company could produce far more than 9.5 per cent per annum, but equally the company could go broke and therefore produce a return of –100 per cent of the investment — a total loss. We can therefore reduce our risk of significant failure by spreading our investment across the universe of potential investments. Diversification is the second risk management technique.

Diversification is achieved by both having a number of investments within each type of investment or asset class — such as shares — and by investing across more than one asset class. If your required return is 7 per cent per annum after fees and taxes over 20 years then you may be able to just use property, which has lower uncertainty than shares. Better yet, you can generate even more diversification and less risk by broadening your universe of investment options to a combination of riskier assets like shares and property with some less risky options like cash and fixed interest.

Investment managers and asset consultants spend enormous amounts of money and intellectual capital in the development of products and services that help investors target a particular level of investment return, over a particular time frame, for a minimum amount of risk.

## Compounding risk

While we have talked about the inherent risks associated with the standard investments available to superannuation users, there are ways that you can compound those risks or make the risks higher. Sometimes this compounding can happen inadvertently.

## Myopic vision

For many people superannuation is treated completely separately to their other investments. In essence, superannuation is a low-tax investment and it should be treated as part of your overall financial security plan. If you don't treat your superannuation as part of your overall retirement plan and strategy then you can run the risk of having unnecessary risk within your financial plan.

For example, if your plan is developed without reference to the value and equity available to you at retirement through your own home or an investment property, you may believe that you need to accrue a higher level of superannuation than is actually necessary to meet your lifestyle requirements. This belief may in turn push you to invest your superannuation in such a way that you take on more risk than is necessary.

In addition, because of superannuation's tax concessions, there may be some advantage in having your super fund contain the assets that have the highest rates of tax applicable. While individual tax situations can vary, the tax for individuals who invest in the various classes of investments will generally look something like this:

| | |
|---|---|
| **High tax** | Cash |
| | Fixed interest |
| | International shares |
| | International property |
| | Australian property |
| **Low tax** | Australian shares |

A comprehensive financial plan should look at these different tax regimes, and it may be advisable to have some of the higher taxed investments in superannuation while keeping some of the lower taxed investments outside of superannuation. Equally such a plan needs to be mindful of liquidity and access as well. If you need access to some of your wealth over both short- and mid-term time frames, you may not be able to use superannuation for assets that will need to be realised prior to your retirement.

Alternatively, you may decide that your optimal asset allocation mix to achieve your desired investment return is 20 per cent property and 80 per cent shares. If you have an investment property, you may well have a very high proportion of property when this is considered in light of all of your assets. You should therefore take into account the value of that property in respect of your total investment portfolio — including superannuation — before you set the asset allocation for your superannuation investments.

In essence, a full and comprehensive financial plan — one that takes into account all of your major financial objectives and time frames, as well as tax considerations — can be a complicated and important piece of work.

## Debt and gearing

Debt can be a great tool to ramp up the effectiveness of your investments, but equally debt will ramp up the losses of investments should the investments prove unsuccessful. Most of the horror stories that played out in the 2008 financial crisis were compounded by debt.

It is always important to understand that debt needs to be carefully managed, especially in terms of servicing the debt; that is, the payment of the interest cost on the debt. A particularly good test to apply to any consideration of debt is whether that debt can be serviced by your normal income, or does it require the income from the investment securing the debt in order to service the interest costs? If it requires some of the investment's income then you need to be realistic about how secure that income is going to be.

Purchasing a residential investment property traditionally uses the rental income from the property to partly pay for the servicing of the debt. The concept of negative gearing means that the costs of the interest on the debt and the maintenance of the property will be greater than the income generated through rent. This effectively means that the house or unit is generating a cash flow loss, which you hope will be offset by future gains in the value of the property. This cash flow loss still has to be covered by other forms of income — usually your pay.

With an investment property, most banks are happy to use the property being purchased as the security for the investment, provided you can demonstrate the ability to service the loan and that you are seeking debt of less than 90 per cent of the value of the property. From the bank's point of view, the value of that property doesn't change substantially simply because it is not actively testing that value. Provided the loan repayments are met everyone stays happy.

Using debt to invest in shares is exactly the same in principle. The major difference is that there are some alternative ways of securing the debt.

### *Home equity as security*

You can borrow against the equity in your home. This means that the home is the security for the debt and you still need to service the interest costs from whatever sources are available to you, usually a combination of your regular salary and the dividends or distributions paid by your investments. That said, if you are increasing the loan limit in order to invest in shares, the bank will not usually include estimates of the investment's dividend or distribution income in its assessment of whether you have sufficient income to service the new loan limit. The bank will usually limit the loan to the lower of 80 per cent of the value of the house and your repayment servicing capacity from your employment income only.

If the value of your investment falls, the bank is not concerned because their security on the loan is your house. You also need to ensure that the home equity loan is structured so that the interest is tax deductible.

## *Margin loans*

You can use a margin loan. These loans use the investments that you are borrowing for as the security for the loan. These loans come with strictly enforced loan-to-value limits. The lender may only lend, say, 70 per cent of the value of a particular company or managed fund as an investment. The other 30 per cent of the portfolio has to be supplied by you.

If the value of that investment falls and this fall then means that the debt is higher than the 70 per cent loan limit for that investment, the lender will ask you to either pay back some of the loan or provide additional shares or units as collateral. If you can't make these payments or additional investments within, say, a week (or sometimes even 24 hours), the lender can sell some of your investments and keep the proceeds of sale as a way of reducing the debt level back to the required amount. This is known as a 'margin call'.

One of the problems with margin calls is that if a sale of the asset is required, that sale is usually occurring during a time of falling prices — not the time that you will generally want to sell the investment.

Margin loans are therefore best used when you can invest in such a way that you have either a significant buffer compared to the loan limit or significant cash flow that would allow for additional investment if needed. For example, if the loan limit is 70 per cent of the value of the share, an appropriate buffer may be to only borrow 50 per cent of the value of the investment. The value of that investment would then have to fall by nearly 30 per cent before a margin call would occur.

Such an approach would work most of the time, but 2008 wasn't a normal year. The falls in the investment markets in 2008 were of such magnitude that margin calls happened for even conservative margin lending arrangements.

## *Double gearing*

Double gearing can occur when you borrow against an existing asset such as your home, and use that debt as a deposit for another investment loan. Clearly things can go horribly wrong in this situation if the performance of the investment is not in line with your expectations.

Imagine a situation where you decide that you want to have an investment portfolio of, say, $1 million. You currently have no substantial assets other than your own home which is worth $1 million, and you have a $400 000 mortgage on that property.

One way to secure that $1 million investment portfolio is to approach your bank and ask them to increase your home loan to the maximum of, say, $800 000. Provided that your income can service the repayments, the bank will generally accept this loan increase.

The additional $400 000 that you have borrowed on your home can then be used as a deposit on an investment portfolio. You could then use a margin loan to fund the purchase of the remaining $600 000 to complete the purchase of your $1 million investment portfolio. It is important to remember that the margin lender doesn't care whether your 40 per cent deposit is freehold equity, or — as is the case here — funded by debt. The margin lender will consider the $400 000 as your 'equity' independent of how it was funded.

Provided that you can service all of the debt and the investment portfolio increases in value at a rate greater than the after-tax cost of the debt then this approach will make you money.

Now let's say that the margin loan limit is 70 per cent of the value of the investment portfolio. At the start of the investment your $600 000 margin loan out of the $1 million investment portfolio means that you are well within the margin loan limit.

If the value of the investment portfolio declined by, say, 30 per cent during a major market correction, the total value of your investment portfolio falls from $1 million to $700 000. The margin loan stays at $600 000, and as a consequence of this your 'equity' in the investment portfolio would fall from $400 000 to $100 000.

As the $600 000 margin loan now represents 86 per cent of the value of the $700 000 investment portfolio, your margin loan now exceeds the 70 per cent loan limit. You would then be in margin call on the margin loan. Your margin lender will send you a polite but strongly worded letter requiring you to correct this situation very quickly.

You would then have two options to get the loan back within the 70 per cent limit:

- ⇨ Pay back $110 000 of the margin loan, which would bring the loan down to $490 000 or 70 per cent of the value of the $700 000 portfolio.
- ⇨ Provide additional similar investments worth $260 000 to bring the total value of the investment portfolio up to $860 000. This would mean that the loan of $600 000 is 70 per cent of the $860 000 value of the portfolio.

Either way, you need to find a very substantial additional amount of money or other collateral very quickly, and if you have borrowed to the limit you may not be able to find the extra money required to cover the margin call. In this case the margin lender will force the sale of some of your investment portfolio and use the proceeds to pay down some of the margin loan, so that loan is back within the 70 per cent loan limit.

Of course the real consequence of this market correction is even worse because you borrowed the deposit for the margin loan. If you had to get out of this arrangement and sell down all of your investments, you would be able to sell your investments now for only $700 000. After paying back the margin loan you would have $100 000 left—which you would then use to repay some of your home loan. The upshot of this investment is that you are back to a position of having a home but you now owe $700 000 rather than $400 000.

You can see that this type of double gearing can lead to situations where people not only lose all of their investments but potentially their home as well.

## Options for controlling risk

Ultimately the best way to control risk is to make sure that each investment decision you make is consistent with your overall investment plan. As we have already seen, your investment plan should take into account the three fundamentals of goals, time frames and risk tolerance. Every time that you make a new investment decision—whether that is to invest more, to pull some money out of your investments or to change existing investments—you should check that this decision is consistent with the three fundamentals of your investment plan.

Problems can start to occur if you feel that you have to act and make changes to the investments because short-term performance is not going to plan. Don't get bulldozed into taking on more risk with your investments in order to catch up to the plan after periods of worse than expected performance. Similarly, make sure you de-risk your portfolio if your regular review shows that you have managed to get ahead of plan.

# Chapter 9

## How to keep the baby when you throw out the bath water

On the day that you are reading this, you don't know if it is a good day or a bad day to invest. You do know that this uncertainty will not change tomorrow or the next day. What will change with certainty is that tomorrow you will have one less day to allow your investment plans to work.

## Do something ... anything

One of the many things that the Global Financial Crisis of 2008/09 has taught us (again) is that markets don't follow predictable patterns. In the wake of shocks like this there is naturally going to be a very strong urge to *do something*, because doing nothing seems like the wrong thing.

It's a bit like a child getting a vaccination. You as a parent know that this will almost certainly be good for the child in the long term, but at the time of the injection your child is obviously being hurt and wants the hurt to go away. Even worse for the parent is that look your child gives you that effectively says *how can you let this happen? Make it stop!*

One of the hardest things to do when your superannuation and your investments are hurting is to look past the short-term hurt, sit on your hands and do nothing, if doing nothing — or rather sticking to the long-term plan — is the right thing to do.

Sometimes, the *do something . . . anything* strategy can actually compound the short-term pain.

## To be or not to be . . . a market timer

Modern financial planning does not try to predict the timing of the ups and downs of markets. Instead, it uses assumptions about long-term rates of investment returns to then build a plan for clients. The fundamentals of the resulting strategy will be how much to invest and for how long, using particular types of investments.

What this means is that financial planners don't usually advise clients that they need to get out of markets at particular times, even if there is some anecdotal commentary that markets may be about to experience a period of lower or negative returns over the short term. Financial planners do, on the other hand, generally advise clients to invest, no matter what the prevailing market conditions. The methodology of investing — whether as a lump sum or through a drip feed or dollar cost averaging approach —

may be different depending upon the stage of the market cycle and the client's attitudes to risk.

The reason for the general advice being to invest no matter what stage of the cycle is that you generally don't know with certainty what stage of the cycle you are actually in. You may be able to claim that you are in a stage of going up or going down but not of one of top or bottom. The tops and bottoms of market cycles can only be determined after the event—with the benefit of hindsight.

Experience and history shows that research and projection tools cannot realistically predict the short-term trends of markets, but financial planners can argue that the future long-term returns of the various types of investment—shares, property, fixed interest and cash—will look pretty similar to the long-term returns actually achieved over the last few decades. As a result, financial planners generally stand by the saying that it is 'time in the market, rather than timing the market' that will produce the best results.

We also know that the *path* of the projections of investment returns used by financial planners and projection tools are by definition not going to be accurate, as shown in figure 9.1 (overleaf)—even if the long-term results are reasonably close to the assumptions used.

Just about every projection tool you see or use will show investments going up over time in a nice smooth way. Sharemarkets clearly don't follow such a path. During 2008, the Australian sharemarket had some daily movements of more than 5 per cent in both directions. The very fact that this sharemarket lost nearly 40 per cent for the 2008 calendar year was clearly not going to be shown on any projection that might have been created in 2003. Likewise a 2003 projection would not have shown the Australian sharemarket going up by over 22 per cent per annum for the next four years before the 2008 crash.

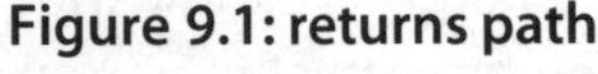

**Figure 9.1: returns path**

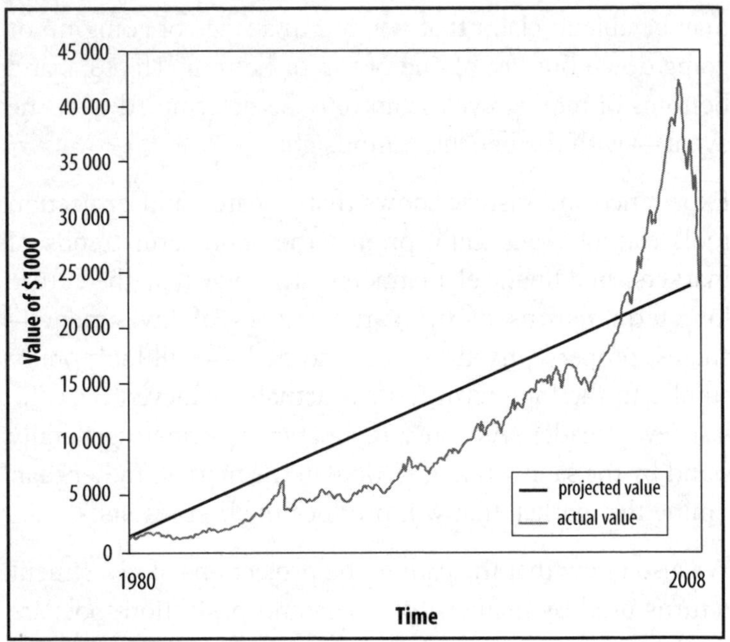


*Source:* Data sourced from Colonial First State.

Even cash investments are subject to periods of volatility. Between March 2008 and March 2009 we saw the Australian Federal Reserve Bank cash rate fall from 7.25 per cent per annum to 3.25 per cent per annum over the year. Returns offered on cash deposits varied by at least this amount as a result.

In the aftermath of 2008, you will probably come across someone, or be told stories about someone, who has 'picked the market' and got out at the right time. The question to ask is whether they got it right last time as well. Whether it was luck or claimed process or not even true, it doesn't matter because you can bet that these people do not have a real process that allows them to get the market timing exactly right *every time* there is a market downturn or a market bounce. Until such a process exists and can be proven, it is best to rely on a process that does work across the long term — which is to stay invested.

So there are two things to take out of this understanding:

- ⇨ Don't beat yourself up if your superannuation and other investments took a hammering in 2008. It wasn't your fault and you could not realistically have foreseen what was going to happen. If you couldn't have foreseen it, why think 'if only I had done something different'?
- ⇨ Don't start thinking that in the future you will be able to see the next big downturn. Nor is this type of unnatural foresight a necessary ability to safely invest for the future.

By going back to the fundamentals of how to invest — understand your goals, your time frames and your risk tolerance — then developing a plan that matches those fundamentals, you will be able to look past the need for clairvoyance.

## Have we seen this before?

The events of 2008 have been a shock for many people. Years of excellent returns have lulled many investors into a false sense of security — a feeling that share investments especially always go up. Despite the doom and gloom that 2008 has generated for superannuation members and retirees, we should try to keep the Global Financial Crisis and subsequent impacts in perspective—especially in terms of a long-term investor's perspective.

A similar event happened following the 1987 sharemarket collapse when the Australian market fell by 42 per cent (as shown in figure 9.2). At the time, it felt like the world was coming apart from an investment perspective, and while it took several years for the market to recover, the world continued to operate and the investment markets eventually powered on.

**Figure 9.2: All Ordinaries index after the 1987 crash**

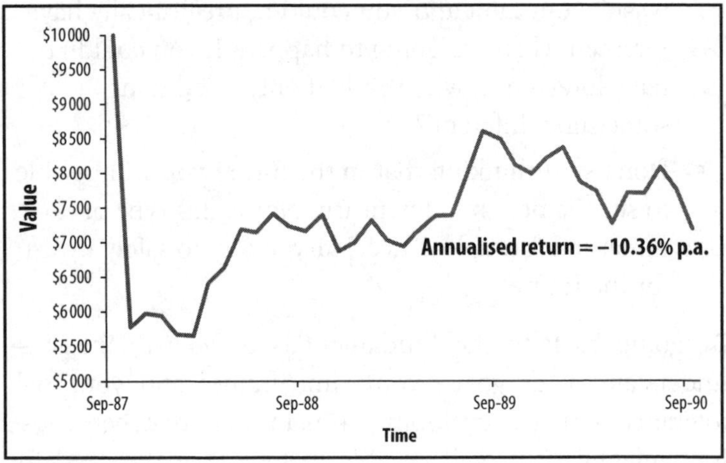

*Source:* IRESS ASX All Ordinaries Accumulation Index/Colonial First State.

In fact, if you had invested at the worst possible time—on 1 January 1987—in an average balanced investment fund with 70 per cent invested in growth assets, the investment performance through to 31 December 2008 would have been 8.8 per cent per annum before fees and taxes. This investment period includes the 1987 sharemarket collapse, the 1994 Bond Market Collapse, the 1997 Asian Currency

Crisis, the 1998 Russian Bond Crisis, the 2001 Tech Wreck and the Global Financial Crisis through to the end of 2008.

## Economic forecasting

Dr Chris Caton is the Chief Economist for BT Financial Group. Some years ago, Dr Caton was presenting to a group of investors and advisers. He claimed that there were some fundamental rules that all good economists tried to adhere to when they were asked to make forecasts.

### Rule 1: forecasts by definition will be wrong

Dr Caton argued that no matter how good your data and analysis of that data, the chance of you getting a forecast *exactly* right was virtually non-existent. Based on this premise, any forecast you made, for at least some level of accuracy, was going to be wrong.

### Rule 2: never change a forecast unless you have to

As a result of rule 1, if you change a forecast, within the term of the original forecast, you will not give yourself a better chance of getting the forecast right. In actual fact, all you will do is give yourself another chance to be wrong.

### Rule 3: only forecast things that don't need to be forecasted

As a consequence of rules 1 and 2, all forecasts should be limited to the best of your ability to avoid any components of the forecast that are uncertain.

A great example of forecasting using rule 3 is held within the forecast that all investment cycles end and start again. Clearly, if you added a time frame to this forecast, you would be in breach of rule 3.

## Rule 4: the best forecast is the one that is the least wrong

In 2000, Dr Caton was among a number of Australian economists surveyed by the *Australian Financial Review* (*AFR*). The economists were asked for their forecast of the exchange rate — where the Australian dollar would be relative to the US dollar — in six months' time. At the end of the six months the *AFR* went back and checked how good the forecasts were. Dr Caton turned out to have the second best forecast, even though he had actually got the direction of the exchange rate movement wrong.

Dr Caton believes that this is a fundamental proof that you don't have to get your forecasts right to be a good forecaster — all you have to be is less wrong than everyone else.

Dr Caton's approach to this is clearly designed to be entertaining and self effacing — he is an excellent economist and his views have been sought-after by investment advisers, media and politicians for decades. The reason for this is that despite the self effacing comments, economists do provide very valuable input into the processes and decisions taken by professional fund managers and investment consultants. These inputs, while never perfectly correct, are more often than not good indicators of the direction of markets and the potential for positive or negative returns out of different asset classes across short-, medium- and long-term views.

His anecdotes and observations about forecasting the future paths of investment markets and currencies do highlight some interesting insights though. There is a logic to the idea that it is difficult to accurately predict the future of investment markets when by their very nature these markets are uncertain.

It is inherently difficult to predict the future, but the process is made even more difficult when it is done at a time of extreme circumstance. In early 2009 forecasting is a bit like standing at the edge of a major highway. If you look to the left (the past) all you can see is a monumental traffic accident. Every form of transport appears to have crashed at the same point on this allegorical highway, and there is carnage everywhere.

In this environment it is virtually impossible to tear your eyes away from the wreckage and look to the right (the future). Ultimately though, looking toward the future is the only thing that makes sense if you want to salvage your superannuation. If you can stand on the side of that road and turn boldly to the right and look forward and ignore what has happened behind you, what would you see?

## Defensive and growth assets

You know that your investment decisions are broadly about move to cash/stay in cash or stay in growth/move to growth. If you are still invested in an option with growth investments at this point you really have to ask, is there any major benefit to getting out now given the extent of the sharemarket falls to date? Also you have to ask if the alternative of cash can offer you anything other than standing still—and you can't rebuild your superannuation by standing still.

It is therefore worth reflecting on what we think defensive assets (cash and fixed interest) and growth assets (property and equities) can realistically offer us in terms of their long-term performance.

## Cash

Cash in many ways is the least uncertain investment type, and yet on the day you are reading this you do not know what the investment return on a cash deposit will be in a year's time. It is clearly not a certainty that a savings deposit you take out today will be paying you 4 per cent per annum next year. You can however say with some certainty that it will probably be between 0 per cent and 5 per cent per annum after fees and taxes.

## Fixed interest

A common query about term deposits is whether they offer certainty around their investment return. On the face of it a single investor can get a term deposit that will pay a fixed rate of return for a fixed period, and when the term expires the original amount invested (the capital) will be returned. In essence you as an investor are actually lending your money to the company that is issuing the term deposit or bond, and in return that company is agreeing to pay you interest on that loan for a fixed term and then to pay you back the loan.

Within your superannuation investment options, this type of investment is called fixed interest. While it sounds like something with certainty there are three main reasons why it isn't:

- ⇨ The actual return from these investments is effectively guaranteed by the company that is issuing the term deposit or bond. If that company goes broke during the term, you may not receive back all of the promised interest or even all of your capital.

- As we have seen, an appropriate way to manage the risk of a single company failing is to diversify across a lot of companies. The fixed-interest investment option in your superannuation fund actually has a lot of different term deposits and bonds—all with different fixed rates and fixed terms—within the investment option, and you as an investor share in these underlying investments. This means that there is not a single fixed rate or term that you as an investor actually receive. Instead you receive a rate that takes into account the mix of rates and terms that the underlying term deposits and bonds pay.
- As interest rates change during the term of the fixed-rate period, the underlying value (or capital value) of the term deposits changes. If interest rates go up, the issuers of the term deposits will need to offer new term deposits at a higher rate of fixed interest in order to get new investors. This means that the existing term deposits—that are now paying a lower rate of return than new term deposits—lose some of their capital value. Similarly, if interest rates go down issuers will offer new term deposits with lower interest rates. The existing term deposits are now more valuable as they are paying a higher interest rate than is available in new term deposits and their capital value increases as a result.

The primary drivers of performance for fixed interest are the size of interest rates in the market and the direction in which they change. In an environment where interests are low and more likely to go up than down over the course of the next three to five years, fixed interest will not do well.

## Property and equities

The uncertainty that exists in property investments and company share investments is higher than cash and fixed interest because there are more and more moving parts to these investments. As the uncertainty of these returns increases, we as logical investors require higher rates of return to accept the higher rates of uncertainty. The whole investment market across all of the different types of investments is effectively built on these principles.

The true insight that comes with this understanding is that in order to achieve the rates of return that you need to make your retirement goals possible, you will need to embrace uncertainty to some degree. We know that markets are not certain, we know that the future is not certain, we know that the best minds with the best systems cannot predict what will happen in the future with 100 per cent accuracy, but if your time frames are long enough you can get a reasonable view of a long-term result.

It is worth considering that if the more certain investment options of cash and fixed interest will lock in failure of achieving long-term goals, what options do you really have? It is not a matter of *if* you need to use growth assets to build wealth, rather a question of *when*.

## The future remains full of possibility

As we have seen, foretelling what was going to happen in 2008 in a realistic and reliable way was not really an option that you could have banked on prior to it happening.

If you have the right plan though, you don't need clairvoyance to be a successful investor. You do need to think